JAILED FOR KENNEDY

JAILED FOR KENNEDY

While owning Dominos and McDonalds Franchises

FRED NICHOLAS CIACELLI

Charleston, SC
www.PalmettoPublishing.com

J.F.K. Jailed For Kennedy

First Edition

Paperback ISBN: 979-8-8229-0661-7

*This book is dedicated to my mom. It is dedicated to all
the moms everywhere who have lost their sons
but remember them every day in their broken hearts.*

CONTENTS

FOREWORD

by
Former Dallas Police Detective James R. Leavelle

Many people in this country loved President John F. Kennedy and mourned his loss, but few exhibited a greater love for him than Nick Ciacelli. No other single individual has collected a larger group of JFK memorabilia than Nick. It was that collection that led us to develop what has become a years-long friendship.

I met Nick in 1991 when he was in Dallas for the filming of Oliver Stone's movie *JFK*. The showpiece of Nick's collection, a limousine built to the same specifications as the one that carried President Kennedy when he was fatally shot, cruised through Dealey Plaza as director Oliver Stone and his crew filmed footage for *JFK*. Nick and I both were among the extras allowed to participate in retelling this important piece of history. I even rode in the limousine.

I had the dubious honor of being part of history myself. I've been through many harrowing experiences in my life. After growing up in Texas and training with the Navy right out of high school, I was working aboard the USS Whitney, which was tied up in Pearl Harbor during the bombing on December 7, 1941. Although my ship was strafed, no one was hurt. We later got caught in a storm with rough waters and I was thrown from a ladder. My injuries sent me to the hospital, which caused me to be released from the service early.

As a civilian, I worked as an auditor for the federal government before joining the Dallas Police Department in 1950. I won't go into the times I almost got shot—as an officer, not as an auditor. But there is one time I don't have to tell you about because it was captured on film for the world to remember.

I was working as a homicide detective when President Kennedy was assassinated.

I was one of the officers assigned to the case. Lee Harvey Oswald was charged with killing both President Kennedy and Officer J.D. Tippet, who was shot 45 minutes after the president's assassination when he tried to detain Oswald. We had more than enough evidence to convict Oswald of both killings had we been able to go to trial.

Oswald was in handcuffs and we were escorting him through the basement of the city jail to be transferred to the county jail. Suddenly, a man burst through the crowd and fired a gun at Oswald, fatally wounding him right in front of me. The man was later identified as Jack Ruby. Photographers captured the look of horror on my face. I was the officer in the big hat.

I escorted Oswald to the hospital and was with him until he was pronounced dead at 1:07 p.m., November 24, 1963. I asked him to talk to me about the assassination. But that's another story.

Nick has heard my stories and the stories of others who were somehow involved in the life and death of President Kennedy. He has collected not only physical memorabilia but also oral pieces of history that he shares in this book.

In 1997, Nick and his wife were divorced. The court ordered him to turn over his collection for sale. He defied the court and spent a year in jail for contempt. I know of no other individual who would do that just to protect his collection. It indicates his love for the president.

While he was in jail, Nick began writing this book. It chronicles his life from a 9-year-old boy up to the present day and features the many important people he has met in his travels. There is a lot of humor and some sadness, but it's always exciting reading. I strongly recommend this book to one and all who remember President John F. Kennedy.

James R. Leavelle
Detective, Retired
Dallas Police Department

With Detective Jim Leavelle

Jim Leavelle at my JFK limo

**Jim Leavelle looking
at his suit**

Leavelle and limo at his home in Garland, Texas

Courtesy Bob Jackson

INTRODUCTION

Sometimes an event happens that is so profound, we remember exactly where we were and what we were doing at that very moment. Friday, November 22, 1963, was just that kind of day. Americans woke up and went on with their routines, heading for work or school. We even had a pretty good idea of what we were going to do with Friday night and the weekend. Then time froze for most of us as we learned of the tragic death of our beloved young president, John Fitzgerald Kennedy.

I was just 9 years old. There was no way I could know the president's death would alter the direction of my future. I remember hugging my mother as she cried. To help make her a little happier, I prepared a John F. Kennedy scrapbook for her. I stayed up all night in the basement and glued in pictures from the newspaper so I could give it to my mom in the morning.

As the years passed, I developed interests just like other boys, but not in sports or fishing. I spent my free time studying about JFK and collecting anything that had to do with him. My hobby became part of my everyday life.

I got my first job at the new local McDonald's when I was 15. At age 23, I met Thomas Monaghan, founder of Domino's Pizza, who financed me for a new Domino's franchise in Dearborn, Michigan. When I told Tom about my Kennedy hobby, he said he had been in the Marines and had bunked with Lee Harvey Oswald, the man accused of assassinating President Kennedy.

When I was 26, McDonald's financed me for one of its franchises in Fort Lauderdale, Florida. By that time, Kennedy had been dead for 17 years. Still, I made sure his photo hung in the dining room at my restaurant.

I married early, and my children grew up with my JFK collection. For the 20 years of my marriage, my wife tolerated my twin passions for my businesses and my collection even though she never shared my intense interest in the history of the young president. But when our marriage ended, my JFK collection took center stage as she challenged me in court for ownership. I was willing to give up my businesses and my homes, but I would not surrender the hobby I had built into an approximately 350-piece traveling museum.

The court challenge ended badly. I was put in a county jail for an entire year for contempt of court. Since I was use to handing out Happy Meals most of my life, sitting in jail I was a man totally out of his element. When the guards learned the reason I was being held, they called me JFK instead of my name.

Meanwhile, I started writing this book. I was allowed one yellow legal pad and one felt-tip pen at a time. I went through more than 30 pads of paper and dozens of pens, writing about a dozen pages a day, as I recalled all the people I had met, places I had visited, and experiences I had encountered. All because of my JFK collection.

After serving my sentence, I tried to pick up my life—both financially and emotionally. I worked dead-end jobs. I even managed a McDonald's location I had previously owned. I may have been humiliated, but as President Richard Nixon said, I was not out yet.

I had written to JFK's son from jail. His public relations people scheduled a date for me to meet him. I guess JFK Jr. was interested in what I did and a bit curious. After all, what kind of person serves jail time to preserve a Kennedy collection? But the meeting never took place. JFK Jr. died in a plane crash in July 1999.

I went public with my story soon afterward. I did newspaper interviews and *Extra TV.* They called me "The Man Who Went to Jail for JFK."

I find humor in everyday life. One day when I was talking to an aide of Senator Edward Kennedy I realized that only three people had ever been jailed in the name of John F. Kennedy: Lee Harvey Oswald, Jack Ruby, and me, Nick Ciacelli.

This book is about my journey. It's a journey that has taken me into meetings and correspondence with heads of state, U.S. presidents and their friends and relatives, and the Kennedys—including JFK's mother, Rose Kennedy. I've met movie stars, TV personalities, and other headline names on this journey of more than 60 years, all while looking back at a shining star named John F. Kennedy.

It is said that a person never really dies as long as he is remembered in the hearts and minds of others. If that's true, then John F. Kennedy is very much alive and well in the hearts and minds of the millions who still miss him today.

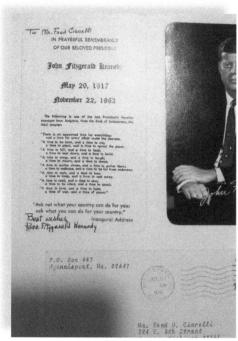

Fred Nicholas Ciacelli,
Monroe News, **1966**

**Sent to me by the president's mother,
Rose Kennedy**

**Front-page news: jailed for
Kennedy collection**

My Kennedy exposition

Jail shoes worn for a year

My McDonalds staff, circa 1982

My mom, Annie, by exhibit items

CHAPTER 1

A LASTING IMPRESSION

It's *exactly* 1:30 p.m. on Sunday, November 22, 1998. Thirty-five years ago from this very minute, President John F. Kennedy was shot to death and I was sitting in a fourth-grade class in Monroe, Michigan. Today I am in jail for a year for contempt of court. A judge ordered the collection of JFK memorabilia I had begun saving in my childhood to be given to my ex-wife and sold off. I refused to do that. You can take away much from a man, even his liberty, but not his passion.

I was 9 years old on the day President Kennedy was shot. My class was studying all of the U.S. presidents that week in November, 1963. The day before, our teacher at Riverside Elementary School had begun telling us about our current president and his family.

I clearly remember hearing my teacher tell us how young President Kennedy was. She told us about his young family, about his father the ambassador, and about how he and his brothers and sisters had played touch football on the lawn of their parents' home in Massachusetts.

It's funny, I don't recall knowing anything about President Kennedy before those lessons, but I became very interested. I raised my hand and told the teacher, "I want to meet President Kennedy someday." I remember her telling me, "That's a nice goal, Fred."

Five minutes later, the school's principal walked into the room and over to the chalkboard where the teacher was standing. They did not speak but I watched the principal motion with her hands for the teacher to come out of the room into the hallway. I knew there was something terribly wrong because of the expression on the principal's face. It was a look I will never forget. She was usually a smiling kind of person, but at that moment she looked like she had been crying. I would very soon find out the reason.

The teacher and the principal were not out of the class for long. After a couple of minutes, the door opened and only the teacher came back in. She stood at the front of the class for a moment, paused, and said nothing. Maybe she could not think of the proper words to say to the innocent faces staring back at her.

Finally, she said gently, "Class, there has been an accident, a very terrible accident. President Kennedy lost his life a short time ago. We are going to dismiss class immediately, but first let's bow our heads and say a prayer for President Kennedy and his family."

After that prayer, my teacher ran over to my desk, hugged me tight, and said, "Now you'll never meet President Kennedy!"

I began to cry, just as I am crying right now as I put these words on this piece of paper.

The emotions today of sadness and loss are no less painful than they were 3½ decades ago. So much time has passed. But on that fateful day, the day my president died, my entire life changed. I went from a normal little boy whose interests were like those of most others, to something special. Hobbies such as football never materialized for me. It was history that grabbed my mind and soul that day.

The day was not yet over. More events followed, and as they unfolded they made a permanent imprint in my heart. This day was going to be buried deep in my soul for a lifetime. For my lifetime and that of anyone who would ever come to know me.

When I got on bus No. 15, most of the other kids seemed as happy as usual. They were talking and laughing. That bothered me a great deal because if our teacher and principal were so upset, shouldn't we all be upset? I didn't understand why the other kids didn't get it.

I sat next to the window, looking out as the bus made its stops. I could not help but think back to the hug my teacher had given me and her stirring words about President Kennedy and myself.

I got off the bus at my stop and ran one block to my house, entering through the side door. We lived in a middle-class neighborhood on a street lined with large Dutch elms. It was a beautiful neighborhood then, and still is today.

I walked through the kitchen into the living room and saw yet another tragic scene. For the first time in my life, I saw my mother crying. She was sitting on the couch weeping, wiping her face and watching our black-and-white Philco television set.

She looked at me. I looked at her.

I walked over and she put her arms around me and hugged me as she continued to cry out loud. I didn't know what to say or how to react. I just hugged her back tight.

She asked whether I knew President Kennedy was dead. I nodded and she cried even more. We both sat on the couch and I asked, "Mom, why are you crying? You didn't even know President Kennedy."

"Everyone knew President Kennedy, everyone loved him. He was such a nice man. He was like a relative to me. And now he is gone."

I began to cry again. Her words stuck in my mind, the idea of thinking of him as a relative. I knew my mom must have really liked President Kennedy.

To see my mother crying was devastating. Seeing an adult cry was something I'd never experienced before. Adults did not cry in front of children much in the 1960s, yet that day I had seen my principal, my teacher, and my own mother crying.

My two older sisters came home and we all watched television together. A few hours later, around dinnertime, my dad came home from his job at the Ford Motor Company. He put his lunchbox on the yellow kitchen counter and walked into the living room. For the first time in my life, when I looked into my dad's steel-gray eyes I saw them filled with tears.

Dads are not supposed to cry. Even boys weren't supposed to cry in those days. I've not seen my dad cry again to this day 35 years later, but he cried the day President Kennedy was killed.

My father told me many years later that he had voted for Kennedy's opponent, Richard Nixon. My father's emotions were not political that day, but personal. They showed a side of him I had not known. President Kennedy made that kind of an impression on people, and my dad, as strong as he was, felt the loss.

My dad was 42 years old when President Kennedy died at age 46. Maybe in his own way my dad felt a personal recognition of the president's loss of his family and his own mortality. Perhaps my dad was thinking that the president, a man who had everything in life, who had so much to look forward to, now did not even have life itself. The day President Kennedy died made all of us contemplate our own futures.

I began looking at the newspaper that day while my family was glued to the television. I saved the newspaper and asked my mom not to throw it away.

On this day and over the next four days of watching television, I realized that I wanted to remember President Kennedy. I guess the way the adults in my life reacted to President Kennedy's death made a lasting emotional impression on a little boy.

That dark day in November 1963 ignited a labor of love and dedication inside me. The people, places, and things I would encounter because of that lasting emotional impression still amaze me.

Riverside Elementary School fourth grade

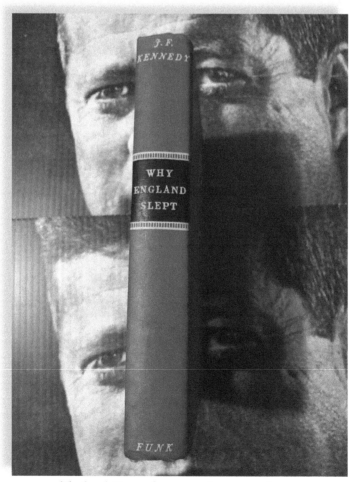

**The book Kennedy wrote, given to me by my
fourth-grade teacher, Mrs. Ruder**

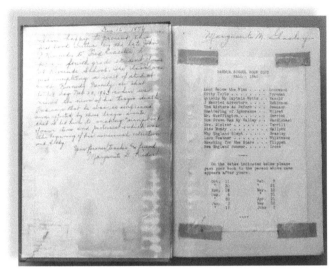

Why England Slept, from my teacher

My dad, Fred, at Original Limo in Dearborn, Michigan

CHAPTER 2

A BUDDING COLLECTION

I began collecting anything I could get my hands on related to President Kennedy. I cut out newspaper articles and purchased magazines with pictures of Kennedy on the cover. I bought stamps, coins, bubble gum cards, records, tapestries, books, models and busts featuring Kennedy. I even began to write to people who had known or worked with the president.

My first letter was written at age 12 to a congressman in Michigan. He sent me a PT-109 tie clip that President Kennedy had given him, along with a letter on U.S. Congress stationary. What a thrill that was. It fueled my interest even more. I still have that letter and tie clip, and look at them often.

I wrote to Mrs. Kennedy that same year, and she sent me a thank-you note with her name printed on the card and envelope. I wrote to her again many years later, and she signed two color photographs for me. I still have the large postal envelopes with her New York address printed on them and those signatures. I even got to wave at her once at the JFK Library in 1979. I'll tell you about later in the book.

When I was 15, I got a job at McDonald's. By then my Kennedy collection was known by everyone in town. Every year on November 22, the local newspaper in Monroe, Michigan, published my photo and listed any new item or letter I had received since the year before. TV stations sent news crews to my house to film my latest collectibles.

People were not going to forget President Kennedy if I had something to say about it. Matter of fact, everyone was extremely interested in Kennedy and my collection. That was no surprise to me because, after all, my mother had told me how much people loved him.

Once I was earning money at McDonald's, I began to get serious about collecting quality Kennedy items. I bought large stamp collections and purchased 1960 original campaign buttons, pins, ribbons, and posters. I sent for Kennedy inaugural medals in bronze and silver direct from the U.S. government. Whenever I watched a television program that had to do with President Kennedy, I sent for the transcripts if they were available. I wanted it all, no matter how small or insignificant an item seemed. If it was related to President Kennedy, I collected it.

My birthday and Christmas gifts always had something to do with President Kennedy. My mother was my greatest supporter when it came to my hobby. She even sends me Kennedy books to read while I am here in jail.

During my younger years, my relatives brought me books, newspapers, coins, and magazines. Strangers would give me boxes and boxes of Kennedy materials, all for free. They said they wanted their stuff to go to someone who appreciated it and would take care of it. Pretty amazing! I always sent them a written thank you on my special JFK stationary that I had printed with my own address.

When I turned 23 and purchased a Domino's pizza franchise in Dearborn, Michigan, I put a large photo of President Kennedy on the wall. That way my employees could share in my unusual hobby and I could keep it near me in some way.

At age 26, I purchased a McDonald's franchise in Fort Lauderdale, Florida. I remodeled my dining rooms in a 1960s theme. In my McDonald's, customers saw a custom-made enlargement of candidate Kennedy vintage 1960 holding a McDonald's cup from that era. Customers loved it. In the lobby, I had a video featuring many 1960s musical artists. With special permission and payment, I was allowed to use the recording artists' songs. In between songs were vintage 1960s and '70s McDonald's commercials. I also included clips of JFK's speeches, remarks, and press conference questions and answers.

The video was a big hit, and everyone knew how much it all meant to me. During my 25 years with McDonald's, customers and employees constantly gave me JFK-related memorabilia. My management gave me a cake for my 41st birthday that looked like Kennedy's presidential limousine, flags and all.

Those were the best times for me, seeing others get interested in my Kennedy hobby.

Some of the students at Fort Lauderdale High School became so interested in all the Kennedy memorabilia after talking with me and visiting my restaurant that they would recall dates in history as "BK" or "AK," meaning "Before Kennedy" or "After Kennedy." Of course, they knew it was a way to my heart and a way to humor me, so I always gave them free sundaes with extra toppings when they got me to talk about John F. Kennedy. Boy, did I give away a lot of sundaes!

In 1979 I wrote to Dave Powers, a special assistant and best friend of President Kennedy. We talked for a few months and exchanged letters and newspaper articles. At the time, Dave was curator of the JFK Library that was being built in Boston. When it came time to open the library and museum, Dave called me to say he was sending me a special handwritten invitation. He told me, "You're Kennedy's greatest fan! So I'll see you there."

On October 20, 1979, I met Dave in person and we had our photo taken together. I was one of the first people in America to see the new Kennedy Library. President Carter spoke, and he received the key to the library from the Kennedy family.

President Kennedy's son also spoke that day. Senator Edward Kennedy made a speech on behalf of his fallen brother. Tip O'Neill, Lauren Bacall, and all of the former president's Cabinet members were on hand as well.

Sitting on stage next to John Kennedy Jr. and Caroline Kennedy was their mother. Jacqueline Kennedy stared out into the vast crowd. She said nothing. She was almost expressionless except for the hint of a very small smile that was gracious and feminine. I remember looking at her in her dark gray outfit. It was simple, and covered her neck and arms. When the ceremony ended, I quickly got up from my chair to go meet her. She had other plans, however, darting out toward her waiting car.

I arrived just before she got inside the vehicle. I looked at her and said, "Hello, Mrs. Kennedy."

Turning her head, she looked at me, smiled, nodded, and stepped into the car.

I waved to her as she drove away, and she waved back.

I wrote to her once after that and she signed my photos. But I respected her privacy and never wrote to her again.

I grieved in 1994 when she passed away. I'll never forget that moment when Jackie Kennedy looked at me and smiled. It was history for me.

It had taken 16 years for me to meet the Kennedy family. After I did, I wondered what else could possibly happen. I was in heaven as a collector at this point. *Where do I go from here?* was my big question.

With Dave Powers at the
opening day of the
JFK Library, October 1979

Pizza delivery with
founder's Rolls Royce

Kids' tour inside my
McDonald's franchise, 1984

With founder of Domino's Pizza
at my franchise in 1977

Me standing in the crowd at the
1979 library opening (center)

One of many local news stories, this one from the
Everette Payette Collection

First McDonald's franchise, Fort Lauderdale, Florida, 1982

CHAPTER 3

A VERY SPECIAL CAR

By 1983, I was not sure what to do with my Kennedy collection. I was so busy working 15 hours a day at McDonald's and raising a family that there was not much time for my hobby. The '80s flew by as I worked my franchise like it was the mission to the moon. I had taken over a location that was losing money and I turned it around, but it took years to do it. Although daily operations and standards were being met, and McDonald's was very pleased with the turn-around, profits were not great.

As I perfected my management and operational skills at McDonald's, I bought two more locations. At age 33, I owned three franchises. The bad news was all of them were well below the average sales nationwide in the McDonald's system. Although cash flow was there, profits were marginal compared with most other McDonald's stores.

I decided in early 1987 to cancel two of my contracts and focus on one store: the original one that had "made me" and had the most future potential. This move would prove to be the smartest decision I would make. One year later, one of my former McDonald's stores closed; the other was sold twice more during the next few years.

I went back to work and built a number one store in sales and profits in Fort Lauderdale. JFK was alive and well on the walls, along with the Beatles, Lucy and Desi, John Wayne, James Dean, and the founder of McDonald's Ray Kroc.

Once I had a hit, it was time to do something with my Kennedy collection.

I had watched a movie starring Martin Sheen as JFK when it was on TV in 1983. I remembered watching the three-part mini-series and seeing Sheen ride in a replica of Kennedy's presidential limousine. Before the movie was over, I was planning to find out who made the car for the production. I wondered how I could get my hands on it.

I contacted the movie production company and found the man responsible for the limo look-alike. Even though I had absolutely no idea what I would do with a replica of a presidential vehicle, I just knew I had to have it.

Marty Martino of Gum Springs, Virginia, had made the car from two 1961 Lincolns. Marty was a prop designer and builder with a good reputation in the movie business. When I called him and told him who I was and what I wanted, the news he gave me was not what I wanted to hear. The car was already sold and had been shipped to a man in New Jersey.

I was devastated. I really wanted that movie car.

Marty suggested the idea of making another car. He said he could make it better and even more realistic. He knew where to locate another two 1961 Lincolns, and he said he would do it for me.

I sent him money and he kept me abreast of the progress on our new project. It would take seven months and lots of money to make another 1961 Kennedy bubbletop Lincoln.

Finally Marty was almost done. My 7-year-old son and I got on a plane to Virginia. Marty had several final touches left to be detailed, but I just could not wait to take a look at my own presidential limousine.

As we walked into Marty's workshop, I held my son's hand. I was so excited. And there it was: the long, sleek, dark limo, already painted and detailed with the array of antennas adorning the back trunk deck. The Secret Service handles had been installed, the custom blue interior was complete. It was a real sight to see.

Marty and I talked for a while about the running boards, flags, and presidential seals. Then Marty said, "Why don't you take it for a ride and let your son sit in the back seat?"

What a great idea! We took off through the country roads of Virginia. I drove fast and my son had a ball. I'm not sure who the bigger kid was that day.

Back at the workshop, Marty told us the car would be delivered to us in Florida in about a month. We flew back to Fort Lauderdale with photos of our ride in the new limo.

About a month later, the limo arrived on a flatbed truck. It did not have the bubbletop. Instead, Marty had built a custom vinyl top to protect it from the weather.

The car was used in many parades in Fort Lauderdale and Miami. I also used the limo to bring Ronald McDonald to see sick children in hospitals. Mac-Tonight, another McDonald's character, rode in the Kennedy limo for the grand opening of a new corporate McDonald's in Boca Raton, Florida. The Broward County Sheriff's Office used the limo for every parade year in and year out. Whenever TV or newspaper crews came to my house, now they had the presidential limo to talk about and photograph. The car was a natural addition to my Kennedy collection, and to my McDonald's business as well.

I had the Kennedy limo retrofitted into a McDonald's vehicle of sorts. I replaced the American and presidential flags with two custom fringed McDonald's logo flags. I even replaced the presidential seal with the McDonald's "Golden Arches." It looked good. The only items that remained presidential were the hand-sewn presidential seals located inside the rear door panels and my Florida license plate, JFK-1963. It didn't matter. Ronald McDonald loved the car.

And so would the U.S. Secret Service, I would soon discover.

One day I received a call from the sheriff's department in Fort Lauderdale. The Secret Service wanted to use my Kennedy car to carry a U.S. senator in a parade through downtown Miami. I delivered the car and was permitted to ride in the front seat, sitting in the middle between two Secret Service agents.

Another time, the U.S. government used my Kennedy presidential convertible for a visiting head of state, a cabinet member from Ireland. The agents allowed me to drive the car, and two Secret Service agents stood on back on the rear step-plate, holding onto those special Secret Service handles.

That day did not go perfectly, however. When I turned a corner too sharply, one of the agents fell off. His knee was cut a little. He was very upset. Then the transmission burned up on the last block of the parade.

This would not do. It was time for an upgrade. But where does one trade in an exact replica of a famous presidential limousine? And, more importantly, where would I get a new one?

The answer would come a few years later, when I sold the car to a collector in Europe and purchased the original movie car I had tried to buy years before.

The original movie limo had been completely rebuilt from the ground up. The collector who had purchased it spent more than

$95,000 to make every detail a perfect match with President Kennedy's car. He had located the original set of blueprints from Hess & Eisenhardt used by Ford Motor Co. to build and customize Kennedy's presidential limousine. Even today the car is impressive as a near duplicate since it was built from the original plans.

After I bought the rebuilt limo in 1988, the car would go on to make its own history.

The Secret Service code name for the original Kennedy bubbletop Lincoln was X-100. This code was used on the radio transmissions and in daily protective detail conversations throughout the Kennedy presidency. The original X-100 was completely rebuilt in 1964 and was retired from White House service in 1977. It's currently owned by the Ford Motor Co. and is on display at the Henry Ford Museum in Dearborn, Michigan.

Strangely enough, I was allowed inside the original X-100 with permission from the museum in 1984. My son went with me, along with my mother and father. We took a photo of my son sitting in the back of a President Kennedy limousine—but this time it was the real one. History again repeating itself. I took basic measurements and hundreds of photographs of the exterior and interior.

This was only the beginning of a relationship between a man and his car. Much would follow including Oliver Stone's 1991 film *JFK*, in which my X-100 would star.

Original X-100 at The Henry Ford,
Dearborn, Michigan

With special permission to sit
inside Kennedy's car

My duplicate on movie set, Dealey Plaza

Discovery Channel, Dallas, Texas

Original McDonalds 1960's road sign next to Kennedys Limo
at The Henry Ford, Dearborn, Michigan.

My Kennedy Duplicate limo at
Ford Worldwide Headquarters, Dearborn, Michigan

Sheriff Nick Navarro, Senator Paula Hawkins inside my first limo in Miami

CHAPTER 4

SHOWING THE COLLECTION

In 1989, I knew it was time to do something more with my collection. My McDonald's was running well and I wanted a change of pace. I decided to build a museum for my Kennedy memorabilia.

I looked at sites near Kennedy Space Center in Titusville, Florida. I met with local builders and with the Titusville Chamber of Commerce on my proposed project. Everyone was very interested, but it took a lot of capital to fund such an undertaking. The projected costs were out of line as I added up the prices for property, land improvements, water, utilities, and construction.

A local builder went with me to the bank with our blueprints. The proposed design of the building was strikingly beautiful, a replica of the White House. Actually, only the exterior looked like the White House—lawn, fountain, fence, and all, but on a smaller scale. The interior design was rather simple consisting of a large area for the memorabilia, a movie theater, a gift shop, and a snack bar, all staffed with Secret Service look-alikes.

It was a grand plan that no doubt would have been a huge success, but the costs to build it meant a large infusion of capital, something I simply did not have. The bank said it would participate if the builder and I could come up with more money.

We couldn't, so we scrapped the idea and I took another approach. I looked for a building to rent in Kissimmee, Florida, not far from Disney World. I eventually rented a 5000-square foot building with a theater. I remodeled it inside and out, using $100,000 from my home equity. "JFK Remembered" opened on Kennedy's birthday, May 29, 1990.

The cost of operating and advertising were immense. The expense turned out to be too great, even with the income from my McDonald's franchise. Eventually, I had to make a business decision from my head instead of my heart. The museum closed on November 11, 1990.

It was a sad day for me. I was terribly disappointed to see my idea come to such an end. The attorney fees for getting me out of the rental contract were staggering. I'd learned a lot of lessons and paid for them dearly.

At 4 a.m. on that cold night in central Florida, the special screws for the Plexiglas bubbletop could not be found. I was shivering as I drove the convertible south on the highway. As I hauled all my memorabilia to South Florida, trucks and cars followed me along the interstate, filled with my life's work on Kennedy. I sat alone in my X-100, wrapped in a blanket and leading the way on the four-hour trip back home.

My museum had died, but my traveling JFK exhibit was born.

In 1992, I was still operating my McDonald's franchise, working as both the manager and owner. I worked long hours, and invested more than $350,000 in a complete remodel of the restaurant. My McDonald's now had a new roof, a new dining room, new restrooms, new tile floors, new grills, new ceilings, and a new playground—and, of course, some new JFK and 1960s memorabilia. It was a success, sales and profits soared.

Since things were good, I took my "JFK Remembered" exhibit on the road. I would travel for ten days at a time. I did five shows over the next five years.

The traveling Kennedy exhibit was an even bigger success than I could have imagined. The crowds of visitors numbered in the tens of thousands. Adults, seniors, and children all came to see a piece of John Kennedy's life and times.

There was a theme to the exhibit, the same theme I had developed for the museum in Kissimmee. This meant there were no assassination displays. The exhibit focused on John Kennedy's life rather than the tragic events that led to his death. This was a planned calculation on my part and it proved to be a valuable asset when reported on by the media and in the talks I gave to schoolchildren, parents, teachers, everyone who walked through my theater ropes to see the exhibit.

I took a smaller exhibit to schools and spoke to fourth- and fifth-grade classes about John F. Kennedy and Abraham Lincoln. I asked the students to write me a short note on what they learned about the two assassinated presidents.

While visiting Jacksonville, Florida, in 1992, president-elect Bill Clinton heard about my traveling exhibit. He sent me a personal letter indicating his desire to walk through the exhibit with me if his schedule permitted it. He didn't make it, but it was a thrill to be in correspondence with the next president of the United States of America.

Other presidents wrote to me about my collection. President Jimmy Carter even gave me a signed copy of the speech he delivered on October 20, 1979, at the Kennedy Library.

All because of my Kennedy collection.

JFK Remembered Museum, 1990

JFK limo with flags of our 50 states

Air Force One and November 22, 1963, tribute room

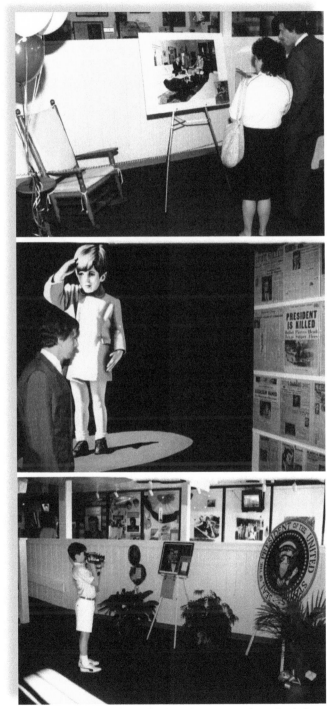

John Jr. mural and inside the JFK Remembered exhibit

**A sign near Kennedy Space Center went up,
but there were too many obstacles.**

August 21, 1992

Fred N. Ciacelli
3410 Leigh Road
Pompano Beach, FL 33306

Dear Fred:

You may have already been contacted by
the campaign scheduling office, but I
wanted to add a personal note of thanks
for your invitation. Your collection
of Kennedy memorabilia looks truly remarkable! I'd love an opportunity to
look over the exhibit with you, but we'll
have to wait and see what my schedule
brings. Thanks!

Sincerely,

Bill Clinton

Bill Clinton

BC:ss

Bill Clinton letter

FOR IMMEDIATE RELEASE OCTOBER 20, 1979

Office of the White House Press Secretary
(Boston, Massachusetts)

THE WHITE HOUSE

REMARKS OF THE PRESIDENT
AT THE
JOHN F. KENNEDY LIBRARY DEDICATION CEREMONY

Boston, Massachusetts

Best wishes
to Fred Ciacelli
Jimmy Carter

11:25 A.M. EDT

Members and friends of the family of John F. Kennedy:
As President of the United States, I am indeed honored to be here
on this occasion at once so solemn and also so joyous -- the
dedication of the John F. Kennedy Library. Like a great cathe-
dral, this building was a long time coming. But it more than
justifies the wait. Its grace and its dignity are, I hope
and believe, worthy of the man whose memory it will nurture.

I never met him, but I know that John Kennedy loved
politics, he loved laughter, and when the two came together, he
loved that best of all.

For example, in a press conference in March 1962, when
the ravages of being President were beginning to show on his face
he was asked this two-part question: "Mr. President, your brothe
Ted said recently on television that after seeing the cares of
office on you, he wasn't sure he would ever be interested in
being President." (Laughter) And the questioner continued,
"I wonder if you could tell us whether, first, if you had it to do
over again, you would work for the presidency, and, second, whethe
you can recommend this job to others?" The President replied,
"Well, the answer to the first question is yes, and the second
is no. I do not recommend it to others -- at least for a while.
(Laughter) (Applause)

MORE

OVER

21 phone calls and several letters to President Carter

CHAPTER 5

MOTORIZED MOVIE STAR

Over the next few years, my collection evolved into a movie business. Oliver Stone called one day and asked whether he could use my X-100 for a film he was shooting called *JFK*. I did not believe a Hollywood studio was calling my office at McDonald's, I thought it was one of my friends playing a joke on me.

But it was no joke.

I put together a contract that included a small part for me in the movie. I didn't get a few of my other demands, like inclusion in the end credits for the presidential limo, but I got the part. And I received a lot more exposure than I ever imagined.

I shipped my X-100 to Dallas and Oliver Stone used it for 28 days. I was on set and took a thousand photographs, working alongside the director and all the movie stars. Once they discovered that I don't drink alcohol, I became the designated driver, chauffeuring them to their destinations after a night of partying.

In the movie, I play a newspaper reporter driving a 1964 convertible seven cars behind the president's. It seemed so real to me to be in that motorcade. I was having the thrill of my life! The makeup artist cut my hair while we were sitting in front of the Texas School Book Depository. A part of history, JFK's and now my own.

I learned a lot from my involvement in that movie. My experience came in handy a few months later when two more Kennedy movies were in production. *Ruby* used my X-100, and this time I was listed in the credits for the use of my car. I also had a role in that movie, and I helped out on the set.

Danny Aiello played Jack Ruby, and we got to be pretty friendly. One night my son Steven, then 14, went with me to Danny's hotel suite to have some photographs signed. Danny told my son about being a movie star and keeping certain values. He looked directly at my son while talking to him. This meant a lot to Steven, and to me.

Later that same year, NBC was making a made-for-TV movie called *A Woman Named Jackie* starring Roma Downey as Jackie Kennedy and Steven Collins as President Kennedy. I had my car shipped to Richmond, Virginia, and the Dallas motorcade scenes were filmed over a two-day weekend.

Once again, I was on set and took a thousand photographs. Steven did not have a driver's license yet, but the streets were empty for the filming. So we pulled my limo out of the production studio and I let him drive while I sat in the back seat videotaping. He had a blast driving down the street in his dad's Kennedy limousine. The flags were flying on the fenders as we pulled up to the studio, where people were waiting to put the car away for the night. I'm not sure who had more fun that time, my son or me.

The X-100 replica now had a unique history of its own with four movies under the hood. My car was a star.

**Director Oliver Stone inside
JFK limo, 1991, Dallas, Texas**

**Actor Gary Oldman playing
Lee Harvey Oswald in *JFK***

**Texas two-stepping with
Lolita Davidovich, who played
Beverly Oliver**

**Actress Lolita Davidovich as
Beverly Oliver in *JFK***

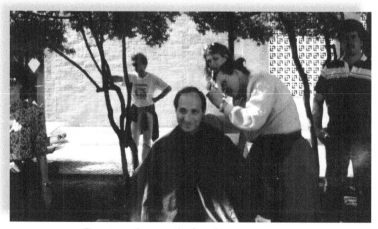

Getting a haircut before being in a scene

Special effects Randy E. Moore (note movie blood on the back)

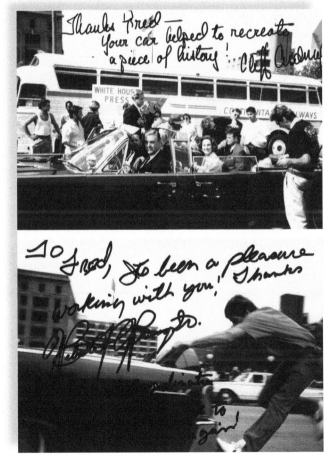

Stunt coordinator Webster Whinery and stunt driver Cliff Cudney

**Mr. Costner sent this a few weeks after filming—
what a surprise!**

Danny Aiello's son Danny Jr. on the set of *Ruby*

**Jodi Farber as Jackie Kennedy in Oliver Stone's
blockbuster film *JFK*, 1991**

Roma Downey, Steven Collins in *A Woman Named Jackie*, **NBC TV**

JFK **Dallas Police Department extras**

CHAPTER 6

AIR FORCE ONE

When George Bush won the presidency in 1988, President Ronald Reagan gave permission for the vice-president-turned-president-elect to fly to Florida in Air Force One. At the time, Air Force One was AF-26000, the plane used by President Kennedy in 1962 and 1963. This was the same plane that took Kennedy to Dallas and brought his body back to Washington in November, 1963.

When I found out Bush was coming to visit his mother, I knew the plane would practically be in my back yard. Air Force One would be sitting on the tarmac at Palm Beach International Airport, not far from where I lived. My mind began to go to work on this opportunity.

On the scheduled date, I made a few calls to find out exactly where Kennedy's Air Force One was parked. Then I drove up to Palm Beach to take a closer look.

When I spotted it on the tarmac, I was thrilled. There I was, once again standing near a piece of history.

I drove back home and picked up my son. My parents were visiting us from Michigan, so my dad came along. We got into my X-100 and made the journey up to Palm Beach.

When we arrived at the gate, I went inside to speak to airport management. I asked if I could park my Kennedy car next to the presidential aircraft so I could take some pictures. They immediately told me no.

Well, I'm not one to take the word no literally, especially if something so important is at stake. This was a once-in-a-lifetime chance.

I gave the management instructions to call the captain of Air Force One. I had brought along my arsenal: personal letters from presidents and the Kennedy family. I told them to ask the captain to check me out with the Secret Service and the Sheriff of Broward County. He did just that and, moments later, flags flying on the limo, we drove across the tarmac to the presidential aircraft.

As we approached Air Force One, I could feel the emotions coming off that plane. A deep sadness, one that others had experienced decades before. There was also an uncomfortable, eerie feeling, knowing that the president's body had traveled aboard that very plane.

I shot several rolls of film that day, photos of my son and my dad, the aircraft and my X-100. I also arranged for a professional photographer to join us, and he took some remarkable photographs.

I already had Air Force One memorabilia in my collection. Earlier that year, while I was in Washington, D.C., attending a convention of McDonald's owners and operators, my family and I toured the White House. Secret Service agent Jeffrey Herzog asked why I seemed to know so much about the White House and the presidency. When I told him I had a collection of President Kennedy's things, he invited us on a special inside tour of the White House complex. Mr. Herzog was a fellow Kennedy fan. He gave us special permits to hang around our necks so that we could go all over the complex.

Agent Herzog showed us the basement, the news conference room, and the Oval Office. As we toured, he introduced me to other staff as a Kennedy collector. One White House staff member gave me so many items from Air Force One and the White House that I needed a bag to carry it all. Many of the items had the presidential seal or the White House printed on it.

I stood at the presidential podium in the news conference room. Then I took my son's photo pointing a finger at the audience like he was taking reporters' questions.

It was so incredible to be there that day and have that kind of proximity to history. I thought I was dreaming, but I have the memorabilia to prove it.

JFK's last doodles on his way to Dallas as shown in my
Florida museum, 1990, and reproduced enlarged on wall

Hand-painted mural by artist Donald Orwell
inside AF1 Room in Kissimmee, 1990

My dad Fred and son at
Kennedy's AF1 SAM 26000,
Palm Beach International Airport

Dad with the 26000

At Palm Beach International Airport, JFK's AF1 with my dad in the front seat!

CHAPTER 7

MEETING THE BUSHES

During President Ronald Reagan's eight years in office, I was friends with Nick Navarro, the Sheriff of Broward County, Florida. I supported the Sheriff's Office through my McDonald's franchise, donating hot coffee and hamburgers to the various charities they supported. They often called me for a short tour of my McDonald's with a meal for the visitors afterward. The guests were usually children from disadvantaged schools. It was rewarding to see all those little faces looking up at me in the back of McDonald's kitchen. I would demonstrate for them how our special mustard and catsup dispensers worked, emitting condiments onto the buns. The kids always said the same thing: "It looks like a flower."

During the next eight years, including the next four years under President George Bush, I remained active with the Sheriff's Office. This enabled me to meet some historical figures, including politicians.

For example, my son and I met former Senator Barry Goldwater when President Bush brought him to South Florida. We both shook his hand and I looked straight into his eyes, thinking of all the history the man had seen. He probably would have been the candidate running against President Kennedy in 1964. Instead, Goldwater ran against President Lyndon Johnson that year, and LBJ clobbered him in the general election. Johnson was known as "Landslide Lyndon" after that one.

That same day I met Goldwater, I was invited to cross under the ropes to meet President Bush. I shook his hand and got his autograph. My son was with me. We were standing along a wall in the foyer of a government building in Fort Lauderdale with only four other people: President Bush, one of his aides, a man in a wheelchair, and some other person. We watched President Bush talking to the man in the wheelchair while waiting for the elevator.

Steven was only 9 at the time. He looked up at me and said, "Dad, how did you get us in here?"

He understood who the president and vice president were, and he knew the historical significance of being there in that moment. I thought about how different his experience was from my own at age 9. Steven had a head start getting a foot in the political world, one I'd had to work very hard to enter.

On another occasion, we met Vice President Dan Quayle. He was in Fort Lauderdale on a campaign trip for President Bush's re-election. Quayle had a striking appearance, very neat and personable. He was articulate, not at all the know-nothing he was portrayed as by the media. He was friendly too. There was a receiving line where he shook everyone's hand before getting into his vice presidential limousine. We got to see the vice presidential airplane, Air Force Two.

Twelve years later, I would own the vice presidential seal that hung above the door in the old executive office building during the terms of Lyndon Johnson and Hubert Humphrey.

I met President Reagan twice when he visited Miami. On one of those occasions, he was at the Diplomat Hotel and I was asked to bring my limo downtown for U.S. Senator Paula Hawkins to use in a parade.

The Secret Service had a parking space waiting for me when I arrived. I parked the limo on the street in front of the hotel, then I went in and met the president and the Bush family, meeting the sons for the first time. When President Reagan made some remarks, Jeb Bush stood beside him. Jeb Bush later became the governor of Florida.

When Vice President George Bush was running for president in 1988, I was invited by the Broward Sheriff's Office to attend a breakfast in Fort Lauderdale. The special meal was held at Lester's Diner, the local restaurant where Bush always stopped to eat whenever he was in Fort Lauderdale. The vice president was not attending the breakfast event, but his son and namesake George W. Bush would be there.

I arrived in the early morning hours so I wouldn't miss anything. I wore my McDonald's tie and jacket because I was proud to be a part of McDonald's. George W. Bush walked into Lester's Diner and was immediately seated right smack dab next to me. I almost dropped off my chair.

I was armed with three leather-bound color photos of President Reagan and Vice President Bush. The special blue leather books each had the presidential seal embossed on the cover. I asked George W. to sign all three for me. And he did.

As we ate bacon and eggs, toast and grits, I kept thinking, *Here I am again, right beside someone famous.* George W. Bush held no elective office at that time. He was not a political figure, not yet. But he would become one, eventually elected governor of Texas twice and, following in his father's footsteps, president of the United States.

After George Bush was elected, I attended my first presidential inaugural. Steven and I boarded a train to Washington, D.C., on

January 17, 1989. The experience I had with my then 12-year-old son is one I'll never forget.

We stayed in an inexpensive hotel. When we arrived, I called our Secret Service friend at the White House. Jeffrey Herzog arranged a tour for us at the White House.

However, I had no tickets to any of the official inaugural festivities. I thought we would just wing it.

We walked to the U.S. Capitol to watch the inaugural parade. It was very cold. Coming from South Florida, we were especially freezing.

Each part of the Capitol grounds is color-coded and numbered, and to enter we needed a special pass. We had no such pass. We were stopped several blocks from the viewing area.

We sat on the curb blocks from the swearing-in ceremony. Both of were shivering and disappointed. So I put on my thinking cap and came up with an idea to get us on the Capitol grounds.

When I spotted a D.C. police officer at one of the temporary gates, I asked Steven to walk over to the nice policeman and tell him that we were father and son from Fort Lauderdale, Florida, and that we didn't have any tickets but could we please come in. I told him, "Point to me so the policeman can see me."

My son was a hard sell. He was very shy and not willing to play along. I'm not sure I would have at his age. But after a lot of prodding, he did it. And when I looked over at the officer, I saw him smiling down at the boy with the bright red hair and freckled face. Then the police officer waved a hand, motioning to me to come on over.

It worked, and we were in!

I thanked the officer for his generosity. Then I looked up his department address when I got home and wrote him a thank-you note.

Steven and I stood together on the lawn of the U.S. Capitol and watched as George H.W. Bush took the oath of office to become the nation's 43rd president.

During the parade down Pennsylvania Avenue, we ran from the Capitol to the White House, following the new president in his motorcade. The crowd was thick so we climbed a tree to get a better view. As we were watching the military bands, I spotted Broward County Sheriff Nick Navarro and his wife walking with the parade. We yelled over to him and he pointed, called hello, and laughed as we snapped each other's pictures.

We walked to the White House to see if we could get a good view of the presidential reviewing stand. As we made our way behind the huge press platform, which was about the size of two tractor-trailer trucks, I spotted the ABC Channel 7 news logo from my hometown of Detroit. I looked like a cameraman because of the cameras and related gadgets I had on my person. I wanted to get some good pictures of the presidential limo, so I told my son to follow my lead and act like I was there as a reporter.

I spotted Jim Harrington from Detroit WXYZ, so I walked over to him, set up my camera, and clicked away.

My son was nervous. He said, "We're going to get in trouble if we get caught up here."

We probably would have, but we didn't. And we only received a few curious stares from the real press.

At the White House, there was a special news facility and viewing stand directly across from the president. It was closed off to anyone lacking the special White House reviewing stand pass.

We had no pass. But we had moxie.

We walked into the white tent set up to house the Secret Service. I laid out my request to all the Secret Service agents in there, and they actually listened. After checking all of my equipment to make sure we were not a threat, they let us in. I saw every news anchor I had ever seen on TV.

The next day, we had a 7 a.m. appointment at the White House. Steven and I arrived at the east gate with cameras, video equipment, and much excitement. Our names were on a list so we went right in after we were searched.

On the grounds of the White House, we walked around, chasing squirrels until we were told to go to the north portico. There, we joined a group of people waiting to go inside the White House. I had never been on this side of the White House before, nor had I entered from below the Truman Balcony. My cameras and video recorder were clicking away at supersonic speeds.

All of a sudden, a second-floor window opened. President Bush leaned out and said hello. He said, "Thanks for coming. I'll be right down."

We went in and took a tour of the White House. It was my son's second tour, but it was not a dull repeat. We vividly remembered the east room of the White House, which had once held President Kennedy's flag-draped coffin. On this visit, President Bush was waiting in a receiving line to shake our hands.

The east room is full of history. During a toast at a state dinner in that room, John F. Kennedy once said, "I think this is the most extraordinary collection of talent, of human knowledge, that has ever been gathered together at the White House, with the possible exception of when Thomas Jefferson dined alone."

The famous painting of George Washington in that same room was saved when British troops burned the White House during the War of 1812. Dolly Madison rescued the painting by cutting it out of the frame, rolling up the canvas, and taking it with them when they fled.

As we stood in the receiving line in the midst of all that amazing history, a Secret Service agent walked over and indicated that we were to take no photographs. I thought to myself, *You've got to be kidding. Here I am approaching the President of the United States of America, who's standing in the east room of the White House, and I am armed with so many cameras I look like a Kodak salesman. And you are telling me not to take a photo?*

When my son and President Bush clasped hands, I grabbed my 35mm Canon A-E1 and shot a photo of the two of them.

I shook the president's hand afterward and wished him well over the next four years. I said, "Good luck, Mr. President."

He just smiled and said, "Thanks."

The Secret Service agent gave me a rather stern look, but I had my photo.

We were exhausted after that and had to board a plane for home. But first we went to Arlington National Cemetery and paid our respects at the grave of President John F. Kennedy.

**Bush day of inauguration;
my son meeting the new president**

Meeting VP Dan Quayle in Fort Lauderdale, Florida

Right up front to see the president

We got in!

VP seal of Lyndon B. Johnson, Richard Nixon,
Hubert Horatio Humphrey

During the 2011 Minnesota State Fair the Kennedy Experience
attendance was overflowing. My long time McDonalds Manager
Mike Potter who helped me set up the show told me if I noticed
that girl staring at the Vice Presidential seal display? Observing
her a while I approached and asked how does she like this exhibit?
She said, "That's my grandfathers"! She was the granddaughter of
the Vice President Humphrey. Everything in this town was named
Humphrey, from the streets to the colleges, and even restaurants. At
this point I gave her an idea. I told her that this seal belongs above
the fireplace mantel in your home. I am only the caretaker for a limited time holding on to history. I told her I did not want anything
for it, just a photo of my presenting it to the Humphrey Family. The
show ended that Saturday. I asked her to please come back so I can
make a formal dedication gift to you on the last day here. We waited
for her and some family to arrive as we torn down and packed up the
collection. She never showed up.

VP Dan Quayle

George W. Bush with Big Mac Be Our Guest—signed too

CHAPTER 8

PRESIDENTS AND POLITICIANS

During that trip to D.C., we visited the office of Senator Edward M. Kennedy. I had been in touch for years with Melody Miller, the deputy family spokeswoman, regarding my collection of President Kennedy memorabilia. So when my son and I dropped by, she let me roam around Senator Kennedy's office and sit in his chair. I looked at Senator Kennedy's presidential flag from the Oval Office that had been his brother's, as well as his World War II dog tags and the inaugural address. There were also loads of other historical items.

After that visit, whenever I was in Washington, D.C., Melody allowed me to look around the office. But I never did run into Senator Kennedy. I do have a wonderful letter from him on U.S. Senate stationery, thanking me on behalf of the Kennedy family for keeping the president's memory alive through my extraordinary collection. And I met him once. I was in my 20s and drove to Ohio when I heard the senator would be there during a campaign for Thomas Luken. I shook the senator's hand and asked him to sign his name for me on a McDonald's "Be our Guest" card. He did, and I still have it.

When I was 20, I learned that President Nixon was going to be in Michigan to dedicate the new Eisenhower High School. I decided to go. He would be the first president I'd ever seen in person.

I drove to the school with my only camera, a Polaroid Instamatic camera. In those days, the camera rolled out a photo right after you took the picture. Then you had to apply a special solution to prevent the photo from fading and disappearing. That camera was all I had at the time, so I made the best of it.

I was standing at a fence in a large group of people. The president arrived by helicopter, accompanied by his wife and Julie and David Eisenhower. It began to rain, so I quickly snapped some pictures, pulling them out of the camera as fast as I could. It was neat to see Nixon since he and Kennedy had been friends in the Senate and had both arrived in Congress at the same time in 1946.

The band played, the rain fell, but I was there with one of the key players in my hobby of collecting Kennedy memorabilia. I still have those original Polaroid pictures. I didn't have the guts at that age to try to meet him and get his autograph. That would come later.

I saw President Carter at motorcades in Toledo, Ohio. I met President Ford in Coral Springs, Florida, and saw him in motorcades and boarding Air Force One at an airport in Toledo. I witnessed President Ford disembark from Air Force One in Toledo as well. He shook my hand at the airport fence and I watched him get in the 1977 Lincoln limo.

During a trip to Washington, D.C., I attended the 1997 inaugural of President Clinton. I saw him through the window of his new Cadillac limo. He drove past me and waved as the motorcade left the White House complex.

The thrill of being close to a U.S. president has not dimmed for me through the years. It's an awesome experience to be in the presence of a person who makes history every day. What has changed, however, is the way I record these events. By the time I saw President Clinton, my cameras and the photographs they produced were of a much better quality.

**Next to John Kennedy's flag from the Oval Office
at Senator Kennedy's Washington office**

Meeting President Ford in Toledo, Ohio

With open-top limo—what a surprise to see this!

Meeting Jimmy Carter at Toledo Express Airport

In Senator Kennedy's office with Kennedy family
spokesperson Melody Miller

Ronald Reagan at the Omni in Miami, Florida;
I was invited as they used my first limo.

Nixon in Michigan in heavy rain;
taken with instant Polaroid camera! Yikes!

Under heavy rain, President Nixon, Pat Nixon, and
Julie and David Eisenhower

Monroe Evening News hometown paper;
credit Everette Payette Collection

CHAPTER 9

A TRANSPORTATION TOUR

In October 1992, I booked my traveling exhibit at the Timonium Fairgrounds in Maryland for the annual fall and winter holiday home show. My friend Mike Potter, who managed my McDonald's store, helped me pack a 21-foot Ryder truck with all the exhibit items and display cases, televisions, signs, and a replica of the presidential podium. The X-100 presidential bubbletop was loaded on a special 21-foot trailer and covered. Then we began the 25-hour journey from South Florida to Maryland.

Whenever the X-100 travels on the interstate, it attracts a lot of attention from passing motorists. Groups of people gather around at rest stops and restaurants. Even though it's shielded by the special custom-fitted protective cover, the limo is recognized by most people over the age of 30. When anyone asked me to please remove the blue cover so they could see the limo better, I complied. How could I not when so many have been so good to me through the years? And who would believe them back home unless they had a photo of the limo as proof?

I plan all my trips to include the stops and delays that occur due to the many interested people. Part of the reason I collect John F. Kennedy memorabilia is to share it with others. I feel gratified when others can enjoy seeing the parts of history I've gathered all my life. I'm also pleased but not surprised at the level of interest people still have today in President Kennedy. I think back to what my mom told me on that dark November day in 1963: "People loved President Kennedy." She was right, and they still do.

So if you ever see me traveling on the interstate with a trailer carrying a big blue presidential Lincoln, have your camera ready. I'll wait for you.

Mike and I arrived in Washington, D.C., around 10 p.m. It was very cold but we managed to look at most of the monuments. We pulled into the Mayflower Hotel about 1 a.m. The Mayflower is one of Washington's finest old hotels. President Kennedy held one of his inaugural balls at the Mayflower, and there are photos of him along the hallways in the main lobby.

That's one reason I stay at the Mayflower when I'm in D.C.

The truck and limo trailer would not fit into the underground garage, so I triple-parked next to the hotel, taking up several No Parking spaces. I figured the police might issue me a few tickets but would never tow a Ryder truck, a trailer, and a 6,410-pound presidential limo.

When I checked on the situation at 5:30 the next morning, I didn't have any tickets on my windshield. But there were police officers surrounding the X-100. Mike was already up and uncovering the limo so they could take a closer look and a few snapshots. The Mayflower front desk told us some police officers went home to get their cameras after seeing the limo on the trailer.

I answered all their questions and snapped a picture or two of each of them standing with the car.

We unloaded the JFK limo and covered the presidential seals, removed the presidential flag. Then we drove around the city, rolling past Washington landmarks. Mike had never been there before and he kept shaking his head in disbelief at all he was seeing.

Everywhere we went, crowds gathered around the limo. People asked questions and took photographs by the hundreds. A group of students from Japan stood by the limo for a class photo, the dome of the U.S. Capitol behind them.

At the Washington Monument, an instant mob formed. It grew larger by the minute, so quickly that we knew we had to get moving before things got out of control. People were touching and grabbing at the limo, they were opening doors and climbing inside. It was a little scary, and happened so fast. I was glad to get out of there.

We drove to Arlington National Cemetery and said a prayer for President Kennedy at his gravesite. But we almost didn't make it out of that parking lot because there were so many interested people mobbing the car. Despite my past experiences, I was not prepared for the enormity of the crowds.

As we were driving on a side street near the White House, a car behind me motioned for us to stop. He waved his hand out the window. When I got out, he flashed his Secret Service credentials.

Boy, am I in trouble, I thought, worried that he was going to arrest me for some law I didn't even know about.

But Fred Claire was not just any Secret Service agent. He was in charge of all presidential protective vehicles in the White House fleet. So he was excited to look at the limo. When I told him that the car was an exact replica, he said he already knew that. His knowledge of the original X-100 limo was legendary within his department. He always sent his new agents to Detroit to take measurements of the Kennedy limo inside and out. He thought it was important for them to see the only vehicle in which a president was ever lost.

Agent Claire loved my X-100. He asked if we could drive it over to the Navy yard behind the Capitol building where they keep the fleet of presidential protective vehicles. He radioed the agents at the Navy yard to expect an exact replica of Kennedy's presidential limousine to be arriving shortly.

As Mike and I drove around looking for the Navy yard, lost in some real bad-looking neighborhoods, we didn't bother to brake long for any stop signs. But we finally arrived and the electric gates opened. We were on our way into history again.

When we pulled up to the small brick building, a dozen federal agents came outside. Agent Claire had said there was an employee who had worked on the original Kennedy vehicle, but unfortunately he went home sick before we arrived. The other agents on duty gathered around the X-100 and asked a lot of questions. The agents lined up alongside the Kennedy car and took turns taking pictures.

The senior agent asked whether I would like to go inside the facility for a tour of the fleet of presidential protective vehicles. This was a once-in-a-lifetime experience. I've always been interested in the presidential cars, and there I was at the center of government where these vehicles are kept ready for the president.

I had watched so much footage and read so many books about presidents that I knew quite a lot about most of the special vehicles. *A Guide to Presidential Travel* had photographs of each president's mode of transportation, from horse and buggy up to the 1970s Lincolns. Now I was able to look at the cars. I saw the custom-built 1960s Lincolns with the special Secret Service grab-handles and the special fold-out rear trunk area. When I asked if I could see what was inside the trunks, an agent opened a few for me. He explained that automatic weapons are kept in there, along with medical equipment, first-aid tools, and a supply of the president's blood type. I wasn't allowed to take pictures, but the agents gave me some souvenir photographs of the presidential fleet.

Agent Claire came by and said, "How would you like the red flashing lights that were on the original car? You can put them on your car, they just bolt on. They're here somewhere."

He asked everyone if they knew where the lights were. He had seen them in a box, but unfortunately was unable to locate those famous red lights.

When I got back to Fort Lauderdale after the fair in Maryland, I sent a thank-you note to the agents. I also sent them a 12-inch, two-pound replica of the X-100 with the bubbletop and fender flags. Not everyone is allowed to look over the presidential fleet, an experience I would never forget.

Marty Martino had made for me 100 copies of a limited edition model of the X-100. These metal models are made from a sand-mold type process, and Marty used red stones that look like the flashing lights on the limo's front bumper. The models are quite impressive.

A few weeks later, I received a Secret Service envelope in the mail. The letter from Agent Claire thanked me for the model. He said there was a window in the Secret Service building that served as a museum, and the limo model and photos of my X-100 with the agents were on display there. I was invited to come see the display when I was back in Washington, D.C.

JFK limo parked at the Mayflower Hotel,
Washington, DC

White House visit at the exact spot
JFK stepped out of his limo; Mike Potter,
my general manager, in driver's seat

Best friend traveling the interstate
with blue custom cover

White House Secret Service garage visit agents and Mike Potter

UNITED STATES SECRET SERVICE
SPECIAL SERVICES DIVISION

TO: Fred Cincelli   DATE: 6/8/93

I regret taking so long to respond to your letter and the wonderful model that you sent me. I have been detailed to investigate the incident in Waco, Tx involving our fellow-Treasury Agency, ATF and I've been travelling a lot.

After clearing things with our lawyers, I transferred your model to our office of Public Affairs. It will be placed in our Exhibit Hall (a poor man's museum) and will be on display there. I felt that it was the most appropriate location for the model. Thank you for your generosity!

Kenny Moko & I look forward to seeing you on your next trip to WDC.

Regards,
FROM: FREDERICK H. KEANE, SAIC   PHONE: 202/566-2877

Great reply from the Secret Service!

US Capitol just before the massive crowds of tourists surrounded us

Cast-art model by Marty Martino

CHAPTER 10

HOBNOBBING WITH HOLLYWOOD

In 1991, during the 28 days of filming in Dallas for the Oliver Stone movie JFK, I met all kinds of people from the motion picture industry. I met Kevin Costner, Sherilynn Fenn, Bryan Doyle Murray, and Lolita Davidovich.

One day when I walked through the high-security area where the stars' movie trailers were parked, I ran into Kevin Costner. He was holding his little girl, who had just arrived with his wife Christine. Kevin was a hot commodity that week in Dallas, where the newspaper had a special column in each issue called "Spotting Kevin Costner." The women went crazy when they saw him, and everyone was looking for a chance to meet him.

Our days in Dallas were coming to a close because the production company, Camelot Productions, was headed to New Orleans.

I walked up to Mr. Costner and introduced myself. He said, "Oh, hello, Fred."

Kevin was aware that the man who owned the Kennedy limousine and a McDonald's franchise wanted to get his signature. However, I sensed that I should respect his privacy with his family, so I said I thought it was a good idea to catch up with him another time. He said thanks.

I never caught up with him again, unfortunately.

He did some scenes at the Texas School Book Depository building at the window on the sixth floor, where Oswald is believed to have hidden while he fired at the motorcade. I met Mr. Costner's look-alike and stand-in, and he posed in my limo while I snapped several photos. So it *looked* like I had pictures of Kevin Costner.

A month later, when I was home in Fort Lauderdale, I received a large manila envelope in the mail. Kevin Costner had sent a black-and-white 8x10 glossy photo of himself dressed as Lt. John Dunbar in *Dances With Wolves.* The inscription said, "Dear Fred, see you in the movies."

What a kindhearted gesture from the star of *JFK.*

I saw Kevin Costner again when I was invited to a party at a Dallas sports bar. Oliver Stone was there as well. There I was, a nobody from nowhere, drinking iced tea with some of Hollywood's greatest talents.

And how did I ever get in such situations? It's simple: I collect Kennedy.

Gary Oldman played Oswald in the movie. We chatted a few times, and one morning when the limo was parked near the door to the Stoneleigh Hotel, he posed for me inside the car.

I met Lolita Davidovich in the lobby of the Stoneleigh Hotel. She played a stripper who had worked for Jack Ruby. Her part was small but significant: the person who could identify both Jack Ruby and Lee Harvey Oswald. She had seen them together at Ruby's nightclub, the Carousel Club.

Lolita and I became good friends, probably because I kept her laughing. Both of us had time to kill, waiting around for our turn in front of the camera. So we ran into each other a lot.

One slow morning when we were in the lobby of the hotel, Lolita said, "Look, you be my buddy. Let's go see some of Dallas together."

We got in a taxi and went to several daytime dance halls. She tried to teach me the Texas two-step, and we danced alongside well-dressed Dallas regulars.

Lolita is Canadian, and on one outing she told the taxi driver to stop at a party store. She came back out with a refreshing soft drink made in Canada.

When I arrived home in Fort Lauderdale, I ordered 25 AM/FM radios that looked like a large order of McDonald's french fries, red box and all. I sent one to Lolita Davidovich. The rest I mailed to the other members of the *JFK* movie production.

JFK film poster

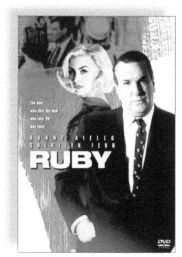

Ruby film poster starring Danny Aiello and Sherilyn Fenn

| Kevin Costner's film double | Actor Kevin Costner in film lot, Dallas, 1991 |

Actress Lolita Davidovich in costume, *JFK*, 1991

With Sherilyn Fenn in Ruby

McDonald's AM/FM French fry radios
sent to main cast and others

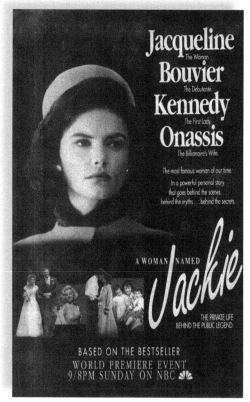

NBC TV print ad, eight-part miniseries

CHAPTER 11

THE OFFICER IN THE BIG HAT

While I was in Dallas, I became friends with James Leavelle. He is still my friend to this day and I write to him and call him often.

Who is James Leavelle? His name is not a household word, but if you were watching TV on the afternoon of Sunday, November 24, 1963, you would remember his face. He is one of the people who became famous for their association with the Kennedy tragedy in Dallas.

At around 1 p.m. that day, Lee Harvey Oswald was being transferred from the Dallas county jail to another jail with higher security. He was handcuffed on his right side to police Detective James Leavelle.

When Oswald was shot in the stomach in the basement of the Dallas jail, the shocking scene was captured by news cameras and broadcast live. The historic event was seen as it occurred on televisions all over America. TV viewers watched as Jack Ruby closed in and pulled the trigger.

The photograph of Mr. Lavelle's facial expression when the tragedy occurred was published in newspapers and magazines all over the world. Oliver Stone secured Mr. Lavelle's unique perspective by hiring him as one of the consultants for *JFK*.

Mr. Leavelle and his wife Tyne and I went to dinner often during the month I was in Dallas. I learned to eat chicken fried steak and Mexican food, both favorites of the Leavelles. He let me ask him all kinds of questions. Jim is a kind man, a self-taught man of wisdom and common sense. You can tell he has a police background because his opinions are clear, concise, and analytical. He's one of those rare people who have a certain regal quality, saying very little but what they do say speaks volumes.

Jim wanted to take a ride in the X-100 through Dealey Plaza, the site of the real-life drama on November 22, 1963. Armed with still and video cameras, we drove the famed route. Jim brought along some of his friends to share the moment.

He took me down the ramp that allowed Jack Ruby entrance into the county jail. He showed me the elevator he had taken with Oswald in the moments before Ruby fired the fatal bullet at Lee Harvey Oswald.

We also visited the exhibit at the old Texas School Book Depository building. We had our photo taken together, standing by a display featuring the famous photo of him with Oswald. When I later sent Mr. Leavelle color enlargements, he signed them for me.

One night I was invited to dinner. Jim said he had someone special for me to meet, plus he was going to show me where Oswald was picked up in Irving, Texas.

We arrived at one of Irving's tallest buildings and went to the top floor where the restaurant was located. I had no idea who would be meeting us there.

I followed Jim and Tyne to a table next to the huge glass windows. Jim pointed out the old Texas theater where Oswald had been hiding when the Dallas police caught him. I'd seen photographs of that theater, and of Oswald being taken away.

While we stood looking at the theater, Jim recounted exactly what happened the day Oswald was shot. I had goose bumps down my back as he recounted the last conversation he'd had with Lee Harvey Oswald. It turned out to be the last conversation Oswald ever had.

Jim instructed Oswald to duck if anyone tried to shoot him, and said he hoped nobody was as good a shot as he was. Oswald said nothing in response, he just smiled. As they rode down in the elevator, Jim said, "Remember what I told you, Lee."

The elevator doors opened and Jim Leavelle and Lee Harvey Oswald stepped out. As the two men walked the few yards toward the waiting police car, Ruby stepped up and fired a single shot.

The bullet hit Oswald's main blood vessel and he bled to death on the way to Parkland Hospital.

Jim Leavelle rode in the back of the ambulance with the wounded Oswald. Knowing the man was dying, Jim asked, "Did you do it, Lee? Did you do it? Did you shoot the president, Lee?"

Oswald did not answer. He groaned in pain, but never uttered a single word.

Famous photo at Dallas jail basement as Ruby shoots Oswald

Mr. Leavell's suite is on display at the Sixth Floor Museum, Dallas, Texas

At his favorite lunch spot
in Garland, Texas.
I got to try on his big hat.

Going for a ride
through Dallas with the
office in the big hat

With Jim Leavelle at his
home office, Garland, Texas

Shooting location of
Lee Harvey Oswald, showing the
basement looking toward the
southeast door to the jail office;
street ramp is also visible

History in my JFK car as we pass
the well-known Grassy Knoll,
Dealey Plaza, Dallas, Texas

Discovery Channel's *JFK: Inside the Target Car;*
Leavelle with Director Robert Erickson

Filming Travel Channel's *Mysteries at the Museum;*
ready to take a ride.

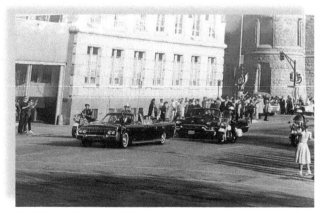

In Oliver Stone's *JFK,* my car making the turn on Elm

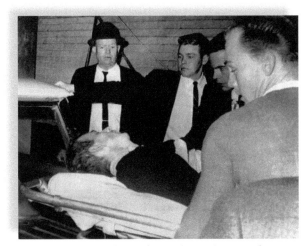

When Leavelle asked, "Did you shoot the president, Lee?"
Oswald said nothing.

I was normally the driver in
most films produced.

Chicken fried steak at
El Fenix, Dallas. Everyone
knew the legend when
he walked in.

CHAPTER 12

THE DAY LBJ DIED

After Jim finished his incredible story, we sat down at the table. It was time now for me to meet Jim Lavelle's other guest.

Madeleine Brown was over 65, a gracious woman who told me she was writing a book about her 25-year love affair.

Her lover: Lyndon Baines Johnson.

The book was titled *Texas in the Morning*. During dinner, she told us many stories and recounted some of the personal conversations she had with LBJ.

Ms. Brown asked me questions about collecting Kennedy. She wanted to know whether I'd ever met President Johnson. He had died on January 22, 1973, when I was 19 years old and a store manager of a new McDonald's. At that time, I was told I was the youngest store manager in the system. I was independent, and had moved out of my parents' home.

On the day LBJ died, he was at his ranch in Texas. I was looking in a mirror, wondering why my face was bleeding. My roommate, Larry White, was also a McDonald's manager. He looked at my face and told me the blood was coming out of a pore near my nose, but that I was not having a nosebleed. It was the strangest thing, something I'd never had before and haven't had since.

I lay down on my bed for a few minutes to help stop the flow. The telephone rang. I will remember this call for the rest of my life. It was the saddest call I've ever received.

My mother was calling from their home in Monroe and she was crying very hard. She said, "Freddie, come home. Your sister has been killed. I need you here. Please come home now."

She didn't want to answer any questions so I didn't ask any. I just told her I'd be there right away.

Before she hung up, she said, "Be careful coming home."

That's my mom, always thinking of me.

I hung up the phone and held the tissue over my bleeding face as I told Larry what had happened. When I walked in the bathroom and looked in the mirror, the bleeding had stopped completely, leaving no sign whatsoever of any trauma on the skin. There was no trace of blood.

I would forget this incident for years. Then one day my mother and I were talking about what happened on that January day. It seems my mother and I may have had some premonitions, each in our own personal way, when my 25-year-old sister was shot to death in her apartment.

On the day my sister was shot, my mother was riding through downtown Monroe with her best friend and cousin Maggie Harvey. Maggie was driving, and she pulled over to let an ambulance pass. My mother remarked, "Oh, you never know who could be in there. It could be one of your kids."

Maggie was a wonderful lady who always had the last word. She said, "Oh, Annie, will you shut up? Don't even think about things like that!"

God works in strange ways. That was, in fact, the ambulance that picked up my sister after she was shot. However, at the time, Diane was not in it. The first responders were on the way to her apartment.

As LBJ lay dead that day, so did my sister.

It was too late for both of them when help finally arrived.

When my mother told me this story, I told her about my bleeding face, and we both had a good cry together.

Some memories we would rather forget as life moves along, and some we cherish until the day we die. Seeing my loving mother cry so desperately at Diane's funeral made an indelible mark in my memory. Watching my mother lean over the coffin, crying out Diane's name, looking down at her daughter's beautiful face, still tears me apart inside. Ten years had passed since I'd seen tears in my mother's eyes for the death of President Kennedy. Now those tears were there again. My mother said goodbye to Diane that day as each member of our family did, knowing that a little part of us had died too.

No, I had never met LBJ, but I vividly remembered the day he died.

At the dinner table that night, Madeleine Brown talked on and on about LBJ. She spoke with incredible detail about her many meetings with Lyndon. She told us what they talked about as he toured the state of Texas with the President and Mrs. Kennedy. It was quite obvious that she did, in fact, know Johnson very well, and that their relationship was well-known at the time, both in Texas and in Washington, D.C.

Ms. Brown described what she was going to put on the cover of her book: two pairs of cowboy boots at the foot of a bed, one set with the presidential seal.

That cover image did not appear on *Texas in the Morning*. But a few years after that dinner, I had in my possession LBJ's vice presidential seal. The one that had hung over his office door at the old executive office building. This seal was used by Richard Nixon too, and by Hubert H. Humphrey.

You never know until after film development—Madeleine Brown,
Leavelle and me against too bright a light at the window

Meeting with assassination witness and taker of famous Polaroid of JFK shot:
Mary Ann Moorman Krahmer with Jim Leavelle

Last photo: October 10, 2013, my mom Annie,
who suffered a massive stroke November 21, 2013

ON THIS DAY IN 1973,

LYNDON B. JOHNSON

SUFFERED A MASSIVE HEART ATTACK AND DIED.
HE WAS 64 YEARS OLD.

His last interview was on January 12, 1973; died January 22, 1973

Mr. and Mrs. Fred L. Ciacelli of
615 Wolverine Ave. announce the en-

My beautiful sister
was shot to death,
murdered in her apartment
January 22, 1973.

Mom, Dad, and Diane about 1947

Me at my big sister's wedding,
Saint Michael's Church, Monroe, Michigan

First Communion, Saint John's
Catholic Church, Monroe, Michigan

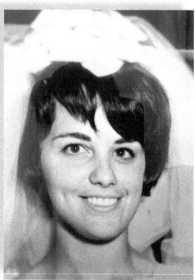

A happy bride

CHAPTER 13

KENNEDY'S AUTOPSY WITNESS

In 1992, I was on the way to Longview, Texas, to show my JFK exhibit. I stopped for a brief visit with Paul O'Connor, the man who received President Kennedy's body in the mahogany casket at Bethesda Naval Center in November, 1963.

O'Connor is a Vietnam veteran who moved to Gainesville in the early 1970s to earn a degree in audiology at the University of Florida. He was wounded in Vietnam, disabled from a back injury.

Paul and I had talked on the telephone multiple times over the previous several months, and he wanted to see my X-100 presidential limousine. Since I had a contract in Texas, I thought it would be a good idea to stop on the way and show Paul the car. I wanted to meet him in person anyway.

Steven was with me so my son and I met up with Paul at our hotel. He was impressed with the car and wanted to see the exhibit, but everything was packed and sealed tightly away in the U-Haul. But Paul was generous with his time, speaking to us at length about his experience in 1964.

Paul's descriptions of the events in Dallas were eerie. He said there were conflicting reports concerning the President's body and the condition it was in when it arrived at Bethesda Naval Hospital. The body entered the morgue two separate times in two different caskets, according to eyewitness accounts. The first entry was at

6:35–6:45 p.m., the body in a plain shipping casket. The second entry was at approximately 8 p.m., the body in the bronze ceremonial casket in which it had originally been placed at Parkland Hospital.

O'Connor said he saw the body arrive in a pink shipping casket in a body bag with the head wrapped in a sheet. There was a massive head wound and a gaping wound in the neck. O'Connor was shocked to see the condition of the body. He said, "The head had nothing left in the cranium but splattered brain matter."

Paul had a surprise for me that day, something to add to my Kennedy collection. Although he knew my collection focused on Kennedy's life, he gave me some photographs that would be a valuable addition to my life's work: a half dozen 8x10 black-and-white glossies of the president's body on the table at Bethesda Naval Hospital. The photos were from before and after the autopsy.

What Paul O'Connor saw on the autopsy table that night in 1963 was not what has been shown in the media. "One picture of the back of his head shows a complete skull and the hair is untouched," O'Connor told us. "But it was all blown away."

Forty years later, O'Connor remained full of doubt about what happened in Dallas. But the passage of time, he said, convinced him that neither he nor anyone else would ever know what really happened that day. "They'll be talking about JFK a hundred years from now, just like we're still talking about Lincoln today," he said.

He was one of the last people to touch Kennedy's body before it was interred. After the autopsy was completed, he helped dress the body and place it in a casket. A Secret Service officer in the room assumed, correctly, that with a name like O'Connor, the young corpsman must be Catholic. The agent gave him a rosary, and told him, "Put it in his hands like you Catholics hold a rosary."

Paul told us, "So I put it in his hands. But there's no special way Catholics hold a rosary."

Afterward, he said, he was "left with a mess to clean up."

He went off duty at 9 the next morning, then slept for 12 hours. When he awoke, he joined the rest of the nation in watching the television coverage of the tragedy.

"We were called into the captain's office to sign orders that, under the threat of a general court-martial, we wouldn't talk about the autopsy," he said. "Then, when the Freedom of Information Act came out, I wanted to get it off my chest."

Among the things he witnessed that night was what he called "the casket switch." While he and the autopsy team were receiving a shipping casket bearing Kennedy's body, he said, Jackie Kennedy was arriving in Washington on a plane with a different casket. "The casket he was put inside in Dallas was not the same one he came to Bethesda in. And I understand from talking with people at the emergency room in Dallas that he was not placed in a body bag. When he got to us, he was in a body bag."

Unzipped, the body bag revealed a gruesome sight.

"I looked at it and said, 'My Lord in heaven.' It looked like a bomb went off inside his head. My primary role was to get the body in and log it in, which I did, and then I was going to remove the brain. But there *was* no brain. Most of it was blown out."

Over the years, O'Connor has talked to others who were at Parkland Hospital in Dallas when Kennedy was brought in. But he received very little information. "I remember thinking, somebody has got to those guys and scared the hell out of them. One doctor, who is dead now, said he was told by higher-ups that he'd better keep his mouth shut if he wanted to continue working in medicine."

Paul said he's been criticized by people who said he was just a young technician, a kid who didn't know what he was looking at during the autopsy. "But I was a hospital corpsman on my second hitch in the Navy, going to medical technology school. I knew anatomy and physiology, and I had participated in 60 or 70 autopsies before Kennedy came in, so I knew what I was doing. All I tell [the critics] is that I was there and they were not."

Although he tries to discuss only those things he personally witnessed and knows to be true, O'Connor has for years speculated on what killed JFK. And, he said, it wasn't a bullet. "I've always said that what killed him was his back brace," he said. "And damned if it didn't come out on TV last night in one of the JFK specials. Kennedy had a bad back and he wore this rigid metal back brace, and when he got hit in the neck, the brace propped him up. If he didn't have the back brace, he would have fallen forward and wouldn't have been hit a second time. The neck wound wouldn't have been fatal. He was wearing something that was supposed to help him," he said, "and it killed him."

When I got home weeks later, I examined the autopsy photos from Paul O'Connor. Looking at them brought tears to my eyes. His death stare was, to me, absolutely horrifying.

I only examined them that once, and it was overwhelming emotionally for me. So I never took them out of my files again, and did not include them in my exhibit.

Navy pathology department official photo opening Kennedy's casket; Paul O'Connor assisted in autopsy, died August 2006

He had tears in his eyes this day when I unwrapped the limo from the trailer.
Orlando, Florida.

Steven, my son, with Paul O'Connor stopping to meet him
on the way to a JFK exhibition in Texas

When asked by a reporter, "Mr. President, how is your aching back?"
JFK replied, "It depends on the weather, political or otherwise."

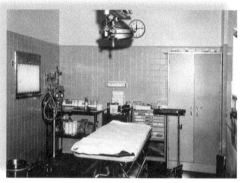

Trauma Room 1, Parkland Memorial
Hospital, where Kennedy died

Room was purchased by the US government, then all contents dismantled: exam-
ination table, clocks, floor tiling, lockers,
trash cans, surgical instruments, gloves,
cotton balls, even a towel dispenser. Today
kept in a six-hundred-thousand-square-
foot underground storage facility also
known as the Caves. The dismantled Trauma Room 1 will be stored there indefinite-
ly. Location: Lenexa, Kansas, a suburb of
Kansas City, Missouri.

The brace that kept him upright
in the limo as he was shot

Kennedy's casket loaded aboard Air Force One; sadly, Jackie Kennedy follows

CHAPTER 14

A VISIT TO THE OVAL OFFICE

On a break from the McDonald's owner convention held in Washington D.C. in 1984, I took my family to the White House. Agent Jeff Herzog asked if we wanted to see the Oval Office. "Are you kidding," I said, thrilled to be on a private tour with my Secret Service friend. President Reagan was back in California for the Easter holiday, so Jeff said we could go in.

As I approached the famous office with my wife and kids, I noted the uniformed US Marine standing guard at the door. Jeff nodded to the man, then warned us not to take any photographs.

We stood behind a blue velvet theater rope that swung across the doorway. I looked at the expansive room, the same room where every president since Theodore Roosevelt had worked. When Teddy Roosevelt decided the White House needed to be enlarged, he had the West Wing built. And this included the Oval Office.

Knowing this was the opportunity of my lifetime, I reached down and turned on my video recorder. I was like a kid in a candy store. I'd read so much about all the presidents, I'd looked at hundreds of photographs and thousands of hours of film of the Kennedy years, I'd studied uncountable pages of material about Kennedy in the Oval Office. And here I was, looking at history with my own eyes.

I pointed out the Remingtons that President Reagan kept in his office, artwork depicting American Indians. My kids got a big kick out of the famous jar of jellybeans sitting on his desk.

Speaking of Reagan's desk, President Kennedy had used the same one. This was no ordinary desk. The presidential desk was made from timbers taken from the English ship *Resolute* and had been given to President Rutherford B. Hayes by Queen Victoria in 1884. On the front of the desk is a plaque which reads "HMS Resolute." The desk has handcrafted ornate woodwork including a hand-carved American eagle and a field of circling stars, the Presidential Coat of Arms. The most famous photograph of this desk is the image in which John Kennedy Jr. is a toddler, playing in his father's office and opening the door with that carving. The photograph appeared in *Life* magazine and was famous around the world.

During one of his presidential addresses from the Oval Office, Reagan said, "This is the same desk that was used by President Kennedy." Reagan had been a Democrat and admired Kennedy. Early in his presidency, Reagan spoke of Kennedy's ability to lead people. He also said, "He's still inspiring people today."

Presidents can choose which desk they wish to use. Reagan discovered that the famous desk used by JFK needed some work, a "presidential fit" so to speak. Kennedy was 6 foot but Reagan was 6'2" so he needed more room. A 4-foot addition was fitted, finished, and attached to the base of the desk.

Reagan had wholesome traditional values. It was said he never removed his jacket in the Oval Office. This was done out of respect for the importance of the room. He chose a desk that would keep an American tradition intact.

Mrs. Kennedy had found the desk while conducting a redecoration of the White House. It had been stored in the basement, and it was her idea to place this "beautiful piece of furniture" in her husband's office.

George Bush had other ideas for the Oval Office. He liked the desk he had used as vice president, so he had it moved into the Oval. Then the Kennedy desk was put away until Bill Clinton was elected.

Clinton was a big admirer of Kennedy after meeting the president in 1963 as an impressionable boy of 16 on a trip to Washington with Boys Nation. After Clinton was elected president, a photograph of young Bill in the Rose Garden shaking President Kennedy's hand was published worldwide. I have a 10x12 photo of that day.

As I stood there looking at the desk that day, I thought about how this historic piece of furniture was back where it belonged. It had a new custodian to watch over it.

Every president has the opportunity to redecorate the office. That's the place where he will run the government during his administration, so the Oval Office represents each man's own ideals and character. Presidents have placed things in the Oval that represent the American public or their own hobbies, interests, or personality.

President Harry S. Truman was a no-nonsense kind of guy. You knew exactly where you stood with Truman; he was his own man, and his own president. On Truman's desk sat a special plaque that read, "The Buck Stops Here." You knew who was in charge of the country when Truman lived in the White House.

One day Truman noticed the floors were sagging. Because of his background in architecture, he ordered a complete rebuild of the interior of the White House. The first family moved across the street to Blair House. The president supervised the construction, ordering that the original wood be saved for future use. He added the famous Truman Balcony on the north side of the mansion.

President Eisenhower enjoyed the game of golf. He kept his putter in the Oval Office. He would even practice putting golf balls in the Oval. When the Kennedys moved in, there were tiny holes in the floor from Eisenhower's golf shoes.

Kennedy kept on his desk a coconut shell. This was the original shell he carved a message on during WWII when he was stranded on an island with his crew. His PT boat had been split in two by a Japanese destroyer. The coconut shell was covered in plastic; he always kept it close by. You can see the shell on display at the John F. Kennedy Presidential Library and Museum in Boston.

When President Kennedy arrived in the Oval Office on his first day, he and his brother Bobby were like two kids, swiveling in the chairs and opening doors to look at everything. At the time, the Oval was pretty much the same as it had been during both the Truman and the Eisenhower administration. The drapes were green with gold stars, the rug was worn from years of service, and the various flags were standing in rows. Overall, the historic room was in need of a facelift.

The entire White House was redecorated during the Kennedy years, every room—even the pool had a new mural on the wall. The Oval office was the last room to be updated, however, and the timing couldn't have been worse.

The President and First Lady left Washington, D.C., on Thursday, November 21, 1963, on a trip to Texas. They planned to be home by Monday to for JFK Jr's 3rd birthday. During those four days, the redecoration of Kennedy's Oval Office was completed. New drapes, new rug, and a new presidential seal, all in red.

But President Kennedy never returned to the Oval.

Lyndon Johnson saw all the red in the Oval Office and it reminded him of Dallas. He immediately ordered the red appointments to be removed. He put the old materials back in place. I've often wondered where the special rug went, but I have not been successful in locating it yet.

President Johnson was intense, especially when it came to being on top of the latest news and information. He had several television sets placed in the Oval so he could watch the news reports—at the same time, on all the networks. The Oval Office changed little during Johnson's tenure. With domestic racial problems and the raging war in Vietnam, he didn't put his energy into a redecoration project.

Nixon had other ideas. He ordered a new rug, new custom drapery, couches and furniture.

Gerald Ford kept the football from his college days on hand. Jimmy Carter eliminated many of the White House and Air Force One mementos bearing the presidential seal. President Reagan was opposed to Carter's austerity program, so during his tenure when you visited the White House or Air Force One, you took home a nice gift with the presidential seal on it.

The Reagans redecorated the Oval with gold drapery. George Bush and Bill Clinton each added new curtains.

Every president comes into office with his own ideals and plans for accomplishments to work toward during his administration. The tradition of imprinting his own identity on his office is repeated with each new chief executive. No doubt that tradition will continue.

After we thanked Jeff and left the White House, I took my family to see President Kennedy's gravesite at Arlington National Cemetery. This is my own tradition. Seeing his grave is always one of my favorite things to do in D.C. The grounds are beautiful. Walking through Arlington National Cemetery gives me a grateful feeling as I think about all the men and women, those brave men and women, who have paid the ultimate price to keep our country free. My father was a Veteran of WWII. He would wear his DAV hat proudly to a meeting or Veteran's Day ceremony.

I felt proud to be American that day, while walking among the tombstones of those many heroes. I hoped my kids would feel the same way.

President Kennedy's gravesite is unique. You walk up a short row of steps to the eternal flame. The plaque there reads: "John Fitzgerald Kennedy 1917–1963." Another hero who makes me proud to be an American.

Secret Service agent visits with me and the famous Lincoln at Whispering Woods residence, Coral Springs, Florida. Took him for a ride to my McDonald's to have a Big Mac!

Lyndon Bains Johnson with Ladybird in his newly decorated Oval Office

Kennedy in Oval Office with Ike's and his office decor

President Nixon with Bob Hope in Nixon's new Oval Office: the furniture, presidential rug, drapes, wallpaper, paint, George H. W. Bush replaced Kennedy's desk. Bill Clinton brought it back in when elected, and it has been there ever since.

President Gerald R. Ford kept the Nixon Oval Office intact

Mrs. Kennedy was to surprise the president with a new decorated Oval Office when they returned from the Texas trip. When Johnson walked in and saw the red, he immediately ordered for it to be put back to the old office of Ike and Kennedy.

Famous worldwide photo of JFK Jr. (John-John). Kennedy had his photographer take photos of his children in his office as Jackie was out of town.

Reagan with new drapes, presidential seal rug, and
new furniture; official photograph

The coconut that saved a president

While at the McDonald's owner/
operators' convention in Washington
with original Mercury 7 astronaut
Gordon Cooper

Before leaving Washington, a visit to Arlington National Cemetery

Leaving a personal tour from Secret Service agent, uniform division

CHAPTER 15

JOINING THE FBI

I've always wanted to work for the US government. Ever since I was a boy, the military and other branches of government have been of great interest to me. This is probably because of my interest in the presidency.

When I started working at McDonald's at age 15, I told the milkshake lady I was going to join the Navy when I got out of high school. An older woman who worked part-time, Elda had a son with a position in the city planner's office. She told me she didn't believe me; she said she thought I'd own a McDonald's someday. So I think it was Elda who put that idea in my head. I had never thought of it before. She told me that all the time, and the concept stuck with me.

But as a teenager, I thought I knew what I was going to do when I got out of school. At that time, there was a lottery for the draft. It was based on birth dates. If your birthday was chosen and soldiers were needed, you were 1-A and on your way to basic training.

I was working as an assistant manager at McDonald's in Monroe, Michigan, when the lottery was broadcast over the radio. The first 50 birthdays would be given orders to report for a physical and basic training. As I listened that night in the back of that McDonald's store, my birthday, December 14th, was announced. It was number 36.

In 1973 the war in Vietnam was winding down. I went to the local Army office and did my duty, reporting as ordered. I passed the physical with flying colors.

I moved to Farmington, Michigan, to manage a brand new McDonald's store. This was my first time living away from home and I was learning to make decisions on my own. I became increasingly self-confident, a vast change from the shy person of just a few years earlier. I was sure that I was ready to go to war, but President Nixon announced the withdrawal of troops from Vietnam and my plan to be in the service evaporated.

In early 1974, I saw an ad for government jobs in the newspaper. The FBI was looking for recruits for entry level office assistants and clerical specialists. An FBI agent lived down the street from my parents. I had moved back in with them that year when I was made manager at a new McDonald's in Monroe.

Paul Costello used to walk by our home as part of his daily exercise routine. One summer evening, I saw him pass by and asked if I could speak with him. I told him about the newspaper ad and said I was very interested. He knew I was in a management position at McDonald's and he was willing to assist me.

Mr. Costello got the application and administered the test. Unfortunately, I flunked. This depressed me, but Mr. Costello gave me some additional help over the next few weeks and I passed the test.

He conducted the required background check, which included talking to my neighbors, the McDonald's franchise owner I worked for and my employees there, my parents, and some of my friends. At 20 years old, I had been working my way up the ladder at McDonald's for four years. I was also a volunteer reserve officer with the Monroe police department.

I was accepted for employment in the FBI in an entry level clerical position. The job was in Washington, D.C. I went out and purchased two new Johnny Carson suits for my exciting new career that was to begin after the holidays in the New Year.

Back in those days, the police took their reserve department seriously. We were involved in many important aspects of everyday police responsibilities. We met once a week, and were required to learn several skills. I purchased a gun and was instructed by the Monroe police department on proper handling of a weapon, gun safety, and cleaning. I was instructed how to fire the weapon at the police firing range. I learned what NICA was and how to use it. My job included dispatch, and I rode in police cars on weekends with a regular police officer.

When I was in uniform driving a marked police car, it was always amusing when I saw a customer from McDonald's. The person would look at me and wonder where they knew me from. This happened often because as a reserve officer I worked at county fairs, church bingo halls, and the city's special events.

I also volunteered briefly in the funeral home where my friend Ray Cotter worked. I would get off work at McDonald's and go to the funeral home to help him clean up. On a few occasions, the telephone would ring at my mother's house with someone from the funeral home asking for me to pick up a body at the hospital. Then Ray would pull up in my parents' driveway in the hearse. The neighbors would look out their doors and windows, wondering what had happened over at the Ciacellis'. At least until they saw me enter the vehicle and drive away. My mother sometimes stood in the doorway watching us go with a memorably sad expression on her face.

One time I was helping Ray vacuum one of the parlors. Everyone had left, and Ray and I were cleaning up after them as usual. This time, however, the body was still laid out.

What happened that night would be a moment that I would always remember. It became a story I would tell to friends and employees over the years. My kids heard this story too, because what happened made a positive impact on my attitude about life.

I had finished vacuuming and was watching Ray go around the casket to arrange flowers. He began winding up the vacuum cord when something in the casket caught his eye. He stopped immediately, reached in, and put his finger in the knot of the corpse's tie. He straightened it, then continued wrapping up the cord.

Horrified, I said, "How can you do that, reach in and touch him like that?"

His words to me were profound. He said, "Ya know, I'm here all damn night and I have to listen to people complain about the weather, their car, not having enough money, the mother-in-law, the job, the boss… They complain about everything and I'm tired of hearing it. That man in there would love to get out of that casket and go stand in the rain with no car, no job, alone and broke. I'm here to help people who can't help themselves anymore, and it makes me feel good to do that. I'm sick of people who have everything in life except a good attitude."

Ray had no idea the impact his words made on me. He'd instantly changed my attitude about life.

From that moment on, the word *attitude* played an important role in my life. In the years to come, I posted signs about attitude in all the McDonald's stores I owned.

Attitude is an intangible product, something you can't hold in your hand or put in your pocket. You can't give a positive attitude to someone, or sell it for any amount of money. It's a quality that we humans have. Positive attitudes can be cultivated in some people, but most often cannot. Either you have a good attitude or you don't, unfortunately. I believe a good positive attitude is more important than all of the other human qualities combined.

If a person has a good attitude, what more can you really ask for?

I'll give you an example. Let's say you have several employees and there are ones who outperform the rest. They constantly meet most or all basic standards and job descriptions and make very few errors. But what if that same group of your best employees doesn't get along well with your managers, supervisors, their fellow workers, or even some of your valued customers? What if the employees who outperform the rest are disruptive in nature, and keep everyone else on edge? The job gets done, but at what cost?

I don't believe job skills are as important as people skills. Unlike a positive attitude, anyone can learn how to get the job done. I'd rather have a person working with me who has a positive attitude and who makes occasional errors or has a little slower pace than a perfect worker with a bad attitude.

After that night in the funeral parlor, I adopted Ray's attitude. And I looked for people who had a similarly positive attitude—for my friends, employees, and girlfriends.

Unfortunately, I was about to meet a girl whose family background and attitudes were the complete opposite of mine. And that ended up being the reason I did not start the job at the FBI.

One day in February 1975, a police officer I was working with told me he wanted to introduce me to a friend of his wife's. The two women worked at a bank together. His wife's friend was in the process of a divorce and had a small child.

That conversation changed my plans and the direction of my life. The FBI was out, and marriage and family was in.

Me, fifteen years old, at home in the kitchen with the McDonald's shirt, giving my dog Duke a treat before I go to work

Monroe Police reserve as I was getting ready to go into the FBI. I actually was accepted, but fate and marriage sidelined that quickly.

CHAPTER 16

THE TODAY SHOW

The 30th anniversary of the assassination of JFK was covered by the mainstream media. New books about Kennedy's life were published, and television specials were aired. Just two years earlier, I had participated in three major motion pictures about JFK, including a TV movie for NBC. So I called the Miami station to see if they were interested in doing a story about my Kennedy collection.

After I sent them some newspaper reprints, a short video of some of my interviews, and footage of my collection on display at various locations, the local station informed me that they were going to do an interview. I would be part of a special edition of *The Today Show* broadcast live from the John F. Kennedy Presidential Library and Museum in Boston.

This was an honor, the crown of achievement for me to be recognized by the Presidential Library for my lifelong efforts.

There were a lot of changes in my life at this time. In November 1993, I was in the process of selling my McDonald's store in Fort Lauderdale. I had owned the store for 13 years, but I was moving to a small town in South Carolina. I was purchasing another store there. The decision to move was based on stress so it was not a logical business decision. My family life was a mess. My daughters were becoming cynical and self-centered, and I thought a move away from the urban glitz of South Florida might help.

All this and more was on my mind at 5 a.m. when the big satellite trucks from NBC pulled up my street in Pompano Beach and parked in front of my house. I dressed in a black Armani jacket and tie and went out to greet the news crew. After speaking with them, I began to prepare the X-100 replica for a national TV appearance.

The custom made bubbletop had to be removed. The presidential and US flags were placed on the front fender in the flag staffs, and the presidential seals embroidered on dark blue material were affixed on the inside rear door panels. As always, the Lincoln limo looked terrific.

For the interview, I was holding something very special. My fourth grade teacher, Mrs. Ruder, was on my mind. It was in her classroom that my fascination with Kennedy began on that dark, unforgettable Friday 30 years earlier. So when the interview began at 7:40 a.m., I had in my hand a 1936 first edition of John F. Kennedy's book *While England Slept,* a gift from Mrs. Ruder for my collection. I visited her many years after I graduated from her class. We had an emotional reunion in her home, and she gave me the book, which she said she read in college. She had autographed and dated the frontispiece, adding a handwritten story about what happened in her classroom on the day Kennedy was shot.

For the show, the guests included President Kennedy's closest advisors and cabinet members: Pierre Salinger, Kennedy's press secretary, David Powers, curator and longtime Kennedy friend and presidential advisor, Arthur Schlesinger, historian. And Fred Ciacelli, the Kennedy collector from Pompano Beach, Florida.

Bryant Gumbel introduced me as the man who had assembled the greatest private collection in the world of the memorabilia of John F. Kennedy. He began asking me questions while the cameraman panned over some of my collection, which I had set up in cases inside my home. (At one point Gumbel referred to me as John, and then said, "I mean Fred.) When he asked what my family thought about my collection, I could answer by telling him about my children's school projects on JFK, for which always received an A. I also told him that I spoke to 4th and 5th graders about President Kennedy when my kids were in the class.

After the interview ended, the station asked me to stand by because Mr. Gumbel wanted to do another interview with me. I asked why, and someone said he does this if he likes you, he must have liked you. The next interview would go out to some of NBC's affiliate stations across the country.

Within minutes we were talking about the X-100 replica parked in my driveway. I explained that the car was used in *JFK, Ruby,* and NBC's *A Woman Named Jackie.* I told him about the special blue paint JFK chose from the Ford Motor Company's samples. I told Gumbel how I would drive the limo in parades, how it was used to chauffeur politicians—and occasionally for trips to the grocery store. He got a good laugh at that.

When asked what the greatest satisfaction in collecting is, many collectors say it lies in showing your collection to others. All the work that goes into collecting is rewarded when others get to enjoy it too. And there I was, showing my Kennedy collection to viewers all over the US.

It doesn't matter how priceless an item might be, or how rare it is. It doesn't matter how much it cost you or if you got it absolutely free. It doesn't matter if the item you collected is as big as a limo or as small as a cufflink. What matters most to a collector is the story, the history that goes with the collection.

All collectors are the temporary custodians of another era, preserving for the next guardian who is out there somewhere. Our pride in our collections is not for the monetary value because true collectors do not collect things to sell them. In today's society, the question is always: "What's it worth?"

Bryant Gumbel did ask me that question. So I told him this: you can't put a price on memories. The real value in collecting is elusive, which is why people never understand the dedication and true spirit of collectors.

After *The Today Show* interview ended, I packed up all the items that had been displayed. I had to finish packing for South Carolina.

What I didn't tell Bryant Gumbel was what I had once told a reporter who asked what my wife thought of me collecting Kennedy: "She tolerates it."

> **You can see the interview at 11.22.1993**
> **https://www.youtube.com/watch?v=0SI1G-nfbog**

National TV live interviews from my front yard on NBC's
Today Show with Bryant Gumbel; Pompano Beach, Florida

Today Show, front of home

CHAPTER 17

MARTY UNDERWOOD AND KENNEDY'S JEWELRY BOX

I received a call from a production manager in California who had just finished making the Oliver Stone film Nixon starring Anthony Hopkins. At the time, I was on contract at a grocery store grand opening with my side hustle, a searchlight business. When I answered my cell phone, the production manager said he got my name from the Oliver Stone people as the person who rented them the Kennedy limo for use in JFK. Now they had a car for sale and wanted to know if I was interested.

The car was a 1968 Lincoln limousine rebuilt by the movie company to look like President Richard Nixon's presidential car.

Of course I was interested, but the only way for me to find out if I wanted the car was to get on a plane to California. I asked them to send me 8x10 glossies of both the interior and the exterior first.

I received the photographs a few days later, and I liked what I saw. I thought maybe the car would be a good addition to my Kennedy collection. Having the Oliver Stone's *Nixon* car was a nice fit. Plus, I could have some fun driving that limo around.

I booked a flight to LA and a hotel room in Santa Monica.

As it turned out, I didn't buy the car. It needed too much work and that wasn't what I wanted to spend my time on. But while I was there, I got to see Mann's Chinese Theater, Hollywood and Vine, Beverly Hills, the Hollywood Stars' Walk of Fame, and other famous spots.

A couple of months later, I had a contract for a weekend search-light rental at a Mercedes Benz dealership just outside Washington, D.C. Normally I would send one of my employees to out of state events so I could remain at home to supervise my McDonald's restaurants. But D.C. was only 12 hours away, and I had a friend in Baltimore I wanted to visit: Marty Underwood.

I brought a fellow McDonald's owner/operator with me on the drive. We were both very busy men. I had purchased my store in South Carolina from Mike two years earlier, and he had just opened up a brand new store. His hobby was golf so I learned some things about golf that weekend. Meanwhile, Mike met Marty and learned a lot about Kennedy.

Mike and I had dinner with Marty, who was in his late 70s at the time. His health was not the best and that concerned me. Marty Underwood was not just any friend. An advance man for Mayor Daly of Chicago, Marty had been hired by Senator Kennedy, and he advanced for President Kennedy. He was also LBJ's advance man, and had conducted 62 foreign and 300 domestic advances for President Johnson.

My life crossed with Marty after a friend of my mother's gave her a newspaper article from the *Toledo Blade,* which she sent to me. I contacted him shortly after seeing the photo of Marty sitting in JFK's famous rocking chair on the cover of *Parade* magazine.

Marty and I spoke on the telephone several times as a week over the next six years. He understood my love for John Kennedy as not many others could. I was able to ask Marty every single question I had ever wanted to ask someone who knew JFK and worked with him. We spent hours on the phone. Marty said he had some very unique presidential items left over from his years at the White

House. He said he wanted me to have some rare, one-of-a-kind items for my Kennedy collection.

So I went to meet him at his house. He was the most generous and thoughtful person. We sat down to talk and he immediately gave me a box he said had been tucked away for over 30 years. The box was full of Kennedy treasures.

JFK's old brown jewelry box had been given to him by his father, Joe Kennedy. A gift when JFK won a seat in Congress. The box was used for the President's and Jackie Kennedy's personal items.

I couldn't believe the contents of the box. Among other items, it contained gold and blue presidential cufflinks, black onyx cufflinks, President Kennedy's Catholic devotional scapular, and the PT-109 gold tie bar he was wearing at his last speech, given on the night before he died.

Marty told me he had secured the box for my collection from the widow of Kenny O'Donnell, Kennedy's Special Assistant and appointment secretary. Marty had told her I was the greatest Kennedy fan he had ever met.

In addition to the box, Marty had other items for me. These included a sweater given to the president on his birthday, which had his initials embroidered on the front; and a gold dagger given to him at a party in Germany by Chancellor Konrad Adenauer. President Kennedy put the dagger in his suit coat pocket, and later said, "What the hell am I supposed to do with this?" It was not reported as a gift because he gave it to Marty.

Marty also gave me an ink pen collection in a glass case. The pens had been used by President Kennedy to sign major bills such as the Nuclear Test Ban Treaty, a mental health bill, and a treaty with Mexico. There were more pens, including the famous Peace Corps pen.

This collection of gifts was huge for me. It meant I had items in my collection that JFK had actually owned.

Because of Marty's generosity, I was later given an award by the Kennedy Political Items Collectors at the John F. Kennedy Presidential Library and Museum.

Pill found in right pocket many years after acquiring JFK's sweater

Shown at my Kennedy Traveling Museum. There was a pain pill in the pocket that I discovered twenty years later after really taking a good look at it—likely for his "aching back."

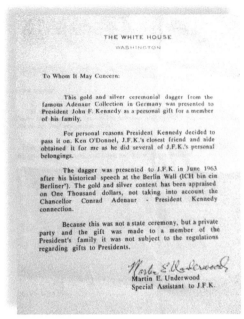

Letter for Marty: from the collection of Chancellor of Germany Konrad Adenauer, who surprised Kennedy as he pulled this out of his coat and wanted him to have it

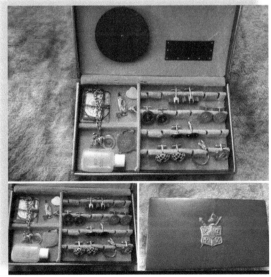

Given to JFK by his father Joe Kennedy when he became a congressman in 1946, winning against Henry Cabot Lodge Jr., whom he later named ambassador to South Vietnam

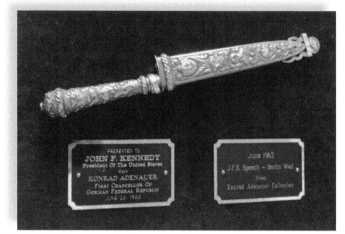

Gold-filled dagger and slip case as displayed at Kennedy Experience

Forged documentation likely

Marty with the Nixons and Connallys. We talked on the phone every day for eleven years and visited with him twice.

Mom was having coffee with her friend in Toledo when her friend said she knew Freddy collected JFK and gave it to her. Mom sent this, and another rare opportunity opened up for me, eventually meeting Marty Underwood!

Dave Powers sent this for the items I had now in my possession. Dave was with Kennedy from the first 1946 campaign for Congress, special assistant with him on every trip, had a room at the White House, became the curator of the JFK Library, and sadly was in the follow-up car right behind him when he was killed in Dallas, Texas.

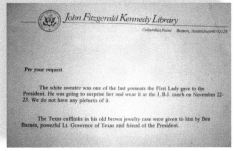

John Fitzgerald Kennedy Library

Columbia Point   Boston, Massachusetts 02125

Per your request

The white sweater was one of the last presents the First Lady gave to the President. He was going to surprise her and wear it at the L.B.J. ranch on November 22-23. We do not have any pictures of it.

The Texas cufflinks in his old brown jewelry case were given to him by Ben Barnes, powerful Lt. Governor of Texas and friend of the President.

Marty with the president on one of his many globe-traveling trips

Visit with Marty in Townsend, Maryland. On the phone with one of his many government friends and contacts.

Sitting in one of President Kennedy's famous rockers at Townsend, Maryland

with fond memories of the time I traveled with you and your father — a great man for whom I have the utmost respect —

MARTY, JR. TALKING TO CLINT HILL ON JET STAR   *Clint Hill*

Marty Underwood Jr. with Secret Service agent and Clint Hill aboard Air Force One from Hawaii

CHAPTER 18

JFK LIMO VISITS THE USS JOHN F. KENNEDY

I went to see the USS John F. Kennedy when it docked in Fort Lauderdale in 1984. I took two of my young children with me. The three of us drove to the port in my first X-100 Kennedy car.

When we pulled up to the next to the USS John F. Kennedy, a crowd gathered around the car. I was ready for this and had some props with me.

The kids and I arranged some large photos of President Kennedy in his original limo, and I set up a poster board with a written description of the vehicle. A Naval officer in the carrier saw what was going on below. He recognized the flags and the presidential limousine.

When my kids and I stepped aboard the ship, the officer greeted us. Then we were given a special tour of the ship. We rode up on jet lifts, and met the captain and his guards.

The officers were fascinated with my collection and the X-100. They wanted a ride in the famous car. I said, why not?

Twelve sailors rode with us in the X-100. We cruised up and down the warm South Florida streets, the presidential flag cutting through the air. I drove to my McDonald's restaurant, and treated them to some good food, good times & great tastes.

When we went back outside, I took a photo of the sailors in their crisp white uniforms, sitting happily in the X-100 parked in front of my store. Then we drove down A1A by the beach, which created quite the scene. All the girls turned to look. They screamed and hooted at the handsome men in uniform as we drove by.

My first-built limo at Fort Lauderdale port with ship ramp in background

Crowds gather immediately to see a presidential limo appear.

View from flight deck; sailors asked for photos.

With two of my children, Stephanie and Steven, on flight deck of USS
Kennedy as we were on a private tour given by one of the top officers.

After my invitation to go for a ride and have a Big Mac meal.
The ride down A1A with spring breaker catcalls, then on for some food!
Fort Lauderdale, Florida.

More sailors wanted inside the limo. They had all they wanted to eat, and we sure had fun. The limo is a kind of national symbol that has a different meaning to everyone. Kennedy's car was built just for him and traveled around the world.

I had fun showing them the limo and feeding them.
The Kennedy limo has opened many doors for me for over 35 years.
You will read later about the door that was closed and locked to me too.

USS Kennedy Sailors posed in front of my Ft. Lauderdale Store

CHAPTER 19

BIG E MASSACHUSETTS FIVE STATES FAIR

The big diesel rental truck was packed with JFK memorabilia, show cases, color TVs, and VCRs. The 1961 presidential replica car was on the trailer, all ready to go. We were headed to Massachusetts for the Big E Five States Fair. This would be the first appearance of the duplicate limo at a state fair.

The car had a beautiful black leather and vinyl cover that snapped on over the Plexiglas. The famous bubble top was nearly impossible to re-create for there was no mold for it and the cost was astronomical. The custom top was built to protect it from the elements.

At the fair, the crowds around the car were enthusiastic. I spoke to the people standing in the long lines, and whenever I witnessed a young person trying to get a photograph of the inside of the limo, I'd tell them to go sit in the back seat. Then I would take their picture. I loved sharing my collection with people born years after President Kennedy's death. It always amazed me to discover a kid who was interested in President Kennedy's life.

Reporters from various TV and radio stations were on hand to do interviews to be shown later on the local news. Thousands of visitors signed the guest book. Visitor counts reached 20,000 a day; over the 18 day period at the fair, we estimated more than 300,000 people came to look at the exhibit called JFK Remembered.

The guest books filled up with the feelings and thoughts so many people were willing to share while they were standing there by my collection. Those books are as valuable to me as any single item in my Kennedy collection. People still loved President Kennedy. Reading these comments brought tears to their eyes. For this reason, I had to keep a box of Kleenex next to the guest book.

My old friend Murray Colen showed up. A former McDonald's manager who had moved back to Boston when I sold my store in Fort Lauderdale, Murray volunteered to help out at the fair. He didn't want any money; he just wanted to catch up with his old boss and friend. I appreciated it because the crowds were thick.

During the fair, an offer was made for me to take my X-100 to Vancouver, British Columbia. The producer of the TV series *The X Files* asked if they could use my car for an episode. When he said the story line was a spoof with JFK as an alien, I wasn't interested. The money was substantial. Still, I passed on the offer. I didn't find it met the standard of respect that I held for my collection.

The state fair introduced me to people from Massachusetts who had actually known John F. Kennedy. Neighbors, people who had hung out with him when he was young. After all, the fair was being held in Kennedy country. I even had a conversation with an older man who told me he once sat down and had a beer with John Kennedy. The man remarked, "He was just one of us, and a really great guy."

---

https://youtu.be/mwk4jDZvQfc

**Place this link in your browser to see the
BIG E Eastern States Fair interview with famous JFK jewelry box**

Nice weather, JFK exhibit draw crowds

'A perfect day for the fair'

By Mark Weiner
Staff writer

Ginger and Frank Price call themselves "fair rats" because they're among a select group of people who visit the New York State Fair several times during its annual 12-day run.

So the Syracuse couple speaks with authority when commenting on the weather for this fair's opening weekend.

"It's perfect," Frank Price said Sunday afternoon. "It's a perfect day for the fair. It doesn't get any better than this."

Mostly sunny skies Sunday and a high of 73 degrees, 5 degrees below normal, provided welcome relief from recent humid weather. It also helped attract large crowds to the state fair, on pace for its third consecutive year of topping 1 million in attendance.

"I would have to say if you would order something, this is what you would have to order for the weather," said fair spokesman Joe LaGuardia. "It's nothing short of spectacular."

Sunday's attendance was 91,548, down 14,346 from attendance on the fair's first Sunday last year. The total for that Sunday in 2002 was a record 105,894.

"You have to remember, last year we did that 105,000 because the previous day was a rainout," LaGuardia said.

Many in Sunday night's crowd took to wearing sweatshirts and light jackets, but the cooler air didn't hurt ice cream sales at one stand on the midway.

"As cold as it gets, you'd be surprised how many people buy our ice cream," said Dustin Motsinger, who served a nonstop line of customers at the Dippin' Dots stand, where the ice cream is chilled to minus 44 degrees.

More pleasant weather is expected for the rest of the week. The National Weather Service predicts mostly sunny skies through Thursday. There is a 40 percent chance of thunderstorms Tuesday night into Wednesday morning.

Viewers recall slain leader

SEAN KIRST
POST-STANDARD COLUMNIST

The line stretched deep into the Horticulture Building at the New York State Fair. Gray-haired men and women waited quietly Sunday alongside of carnival noise, the line had the feel of calling hours.

"He was an amazing president," said Lee Terry, 74, of Interlaken, as a means of explanation. She had just finished viewing "JFK Remembered," an exhibit commemorating this year's 40th anniversary of the killing of President John F. Kennedy.

"I was very fond of him," Terry said. "He had so much ..." Then she stopped, unable to find the words. She raised her hands and made a grasping motion with her fingers, searching for a way to capture Kennedy's vitality, his sense of inspiration.

"He was amazing," Terry said quietly, before she walked into the crowd.

The exhibit was put together by Florida businessman F. Nicholas Ciacelli. It includes one of Kennedy's sweaters and his personal jewelry box. There are campaign buttons, old newspapers, presidential pens and an exact replica of the car in which Kennedy was shot — the same car used in the Oliver Stone movie "JFK."

And there is a prominent photograph of Jackie Kennedy and young John-John — the president's wife and toddler son, somber faces pressed together, both of them now also part of history.

The hushed line made a shuffling circle. You got the sense that people were there less for the artifacts than for the memory. The most powerful moment came at the very end. Ciacelli concludes his exhibit with a

FLORIDA, PAGE B-3

Florida businessman created JFK exhibit

FLORIDA, FROM PAGE B-1

video tracing Kennedy's final hours. It shows the president climbing into the limousine in Dallas. It captures the jubilation that ends with the first shot in Dealey Plaza.

And the video offers a haunting speech in which Kennedy speculates out loud about America's needs in 1990.

Many fairgoers watched in silence, with tears in their eyes. Eleven-year-old Katie Kuney, of Waterloo, put her hands to her face, in dismay. "It's just so disturbing, the way he died, that someone would actually kill him," she said.

Katie's mother, Kathy Kuney, recalled how her Catholic parents were thrilled when Kennedy became the first Catholic president. Still, Kuney's lasting memory is the way that Kennedy was able to make Americans feel for the needs of people beyond themselves.

"He said so many insightful and inspiring things," she said. "I don't even know if people think about 'Ask not what your country can do for you' anymore, even after 9/11, even if it's something people ought to be thinking about."

Ciacelli began working on the exhibit when he was in fourth grade. On the day the president was shot, he said, his teacher began crying. "How many times do you actually see your teacher crying?" Ciacelli asked. "You remember that."

He went home, where his mother was also overcome with grief. That night, to comfort her, he went out and bought every newspaper he could find, and he made her a scrapbook about the president.

In a sense, that scrapbook now covers an entire wing at the state fair.

Ciacelli grew up and saved some money by running three McDonald's restaurants. He became good friends with Marty Underwood, who had worked in the Kennedy and Lyndon B. Johnson administrations. Underwood helped Ciacelli build his collection, which eventually turned into a Kennedy museum that failed.

Undaunted, Ciacelli converted the museum into a traveling exhibit, which he said has been a huge success. At the state fair, "JFK Remembered" is drawing roughly 10,000 visitors a day. There is a line from the moment the exhibit opens at 10 a.m. until it closes 12 hours later, Ciacelli said.

Few of the visitors try to mythologize Kennedy. They can hardly miss the continuing revelations about Kennedy's extramarital affairs, which keep him on the cover of supermarket tabloids.

Yet Kennedy earned forgiveness from the crowd through the raw savagery of his death, and because of what so many of the visitors described as his ability to bring out the selfless nature of Americans.

John and Lucy Shults of Syracuse, both born during World War II, were among those who waited in line for the exhibit. At the end, they stood motionless to watch the video. When the motorcade reached Dealey Plaza, John and Lucy had enough. They turned and lost themselves in the crowd, Lucy gently rubbing her husband's back, until they stopped while Lucy brushed the tears out of her eyes.

"It was his voice," she said softly. "It was enough to take you back."

Sean Kirst is a columnist with The Post-Standard. His columns appear Mondays, Wednesdays and Fridays. Call him at 470-6015 or e-mail him at citynews@syracuse.com.

Local press was always positive when I presented JFK to their city. There were over 350,000 guests who passed through the JFK exhibit in just over two weeks.

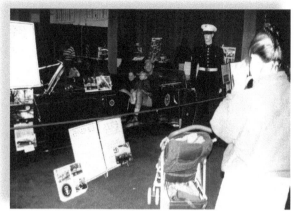

When they ask to go inside the car,
of course I make that happen!

The BIG E is a five-state fair with over
three million paid gate admissions.

Lined up in the rain—surprised even me!

Lined up in every direction to see the
personal items owned by the president.

Many from his home state knew Kennedy well.
Captain Jonathan Maguire drove him, and he said
they talked about fishing, the Navy, and the future.

Attached clear bubble-top unwrapped
after a long drive on the interstate.

Planning, logistics, equipment, and truck rental—
I certainly became sort of an expert.

CHAPTER 20:

MAKING MY MOTHER PROUD

I sat next to my mother on the couch that day in 1963 while she wept at the loss of our president. When she told me that JFK was like a relative, I was confused. I said, "But I'm your son." My mother said that's right, but John Kennedy was every mother's son.

This statement and her deep emotions that day have stayed with me for my lifetime.

When my father returned home later that day, his eyes were glassy. To me, my dad was Superman, but I could see that he too was deeply hurt. A WWII army tank operator with the 11th Armor Division, he had helped to free four concentration camps. His tank rolled over the fences in those horrible German camps. In my eyes, he was made of steel.

Over the next 50 years, my father told me he was proud of my collection but my mother was my biggest fan. Mom would buy things for me at flea markets. Her friends would give her materials on Kennedy, and she would call me every time there was a special on TV or something in the newspaper. She sent me numerous articles on the Kennedys year after year. My mom had grown up in Monroe. All of her relatives and friends who lived there would see my collection featured in the local newspaper every year. So my mother was a proud mom.

During the summer of 2013 when she was 88, I got contracts for what I was then calling the JFK Experience Traveling Museum. I was expected in Novi, Michigan, not far from my hometown. My collection was in ruins by then, so I really needed to rebuild from the bottom up.

I drove to Michigan and spent the summer there with my mother at her home. We went to McDonald's together, we went to the casino. She made me breakfast and cooked the meals I'd loved when I was a kid. I brought hamburgers home in the evening, we ordered pizza, or we had her pasta. Her sauce was fabulous.

My father had died six years earlier, but my mother was not lonely. Annie Ciacelli had a lot of company. Whenever people came over, she would cook up a pot of spaghetti. Or she would slap together some sandwiches, or a snack of cookies and coffee.

Annie Ciacelli always had something to give.

During those three months, I rebuilt my collection and did the Kennedy show in Novi, plus one in Pennsylvania. I had spent $20,000 to rebrand the show, and it was magnificent.

After almost 50 years, my mother finally saw my collection in person at a public exhibit. She came to the show in Novi, and I took her picture at the presidential podium. I'd had a backdrop made to look like the presidential newsroom at the White House. Mom stood at the podium, flanked by US and presidential flags. She pointed her finger and looked at the crowd as if she was the president of the United States giving a speech. She had a wonderful time at the show with my sister Sandy, my cousins, and friends.

On November 2, 2013, I said goodbye for now. I planned to return in February for two more Kennedy shows. I hugged her tight, and she kissed me.

On the 50th anniversary of the Kennedy assassination, I was in Texas. I had tickets to a memorial event in Dealey Plaza which I had been invited by the city of Dallas to attend. I called my mom to tell her I would be in the newspapers the next day. I asked her to pick up a couple newspapers for me at the grocery store.

She said, "Oh, no problem. I can't wait to see what's in the paper."

When I was in Dealey Plaza at 3 o'clock in the afternoon, my mother was in a local grocery store buying two newspapers. Her son's color photo was on the front page of the *Monroe News*. She stood there for a few minutes, talking about how proud she was of son, how he owned the Kennedy car, he owned McDonald's restaurants, and here he was in the paper today. As she walked out of the grocery store, she said, *This is the happiest day of my life!*

That morning, my mother had gone to a Ford Motor Company breakfast with her cousin and sister-in-law. She was planning to go to bingo that night. But when she left the grocery store and started up her silver Ford Focus, she suffered a massive stroke.

The last thing my mother ever spoke about was me…and JFK.

I rushed to the hospital to be by her side. She was on life-support and the doctors told me the damage was extensive. She did squeeze my hand when I told her I was there to take her to bingo. But a few days later, there was no more response. I held my mother's hand as they turned off the life-support.

With one hand on her heart and the other clasped in my own, my mother slipped away to be with my dad and my sister. Ironically, the biggest fan died on Kennedy's 50th anniversary.

My collection was built because of my mother. Now she was gone.

When the anniversary of President Kennedy's death occurs every year, it is also the anniversary of the death of my mother. The loss I feel for the president is now compounded by an even bigger loss, that of my loving mother, Annie Ciacelli.

**I was a mommy's boy and enjoyed all her love she had for me.
I loved to make her laugh.**

My dad Fred and me in Coral Springs, Florida, 1984

My dad in uniform (left). He was in the Battle of the Bulge, 11th armored division, freeing several concentration camps and also meeting up with General Patton's third army.

Thunderbolt framed map hung at the end of the stairs in our basement (above). Looking back, I do not recall ever asking him much about it. He rarely if ever spoke about the war. When I did ask him once, he just said, "We did what we had to do."

My dad at the house he built in 1950 after the war.
With my mom, sister Sandy, son Steven, niece April, and Ashley.

Happy times with my dad in our living room and Honey, my husky wolf dog

Mom (Annie) was my biggest supporter. I will never feel such love again

LINCOLN 111 YEARS AGO — President Abraham Lincoln sits with Civil War General George McClellan at Antietam in this photo taken Oct. 3, 1864, about six months before Lincoln was assassinated. The original photo is owned by Fred N. Ciacelli of Monroe. Mr. Ciacelli reported he bought the photo at an auction in Southfield in 1972 at a cost of $80.

A collector of John F. Kennedy pictures and memorabilia, Mr. Ciacelli said he just happened to come across the Lincoln photo. Lincoln's Birthday is being observed today with city, county and other business offices closed for the occasion.

One of many times the local news printed another story. I sent this to Vice President Hubert H. Humphrey knowing he collected Lincoln items. He replied quickly while in the hospital and died a few weeks later, his niece told me.

One of many advertising pieces for the Kennedy exposition (left)

Fourth-grade photo when my
great interest began
that November day

In 2013 I spent the last three months rebuilding the exhibit. Mom was there to preview every new display. She would see the on-the-road show for the first time in fifty years in November 2013, only then suffering a massive stroke on the eve of the fiftieth anniversary on November 21, 2013.

Agent Clint Hill as he climbs on the rear section of the Kennedy Lincoln. The *only* agent to react to the shooting.

She was thrilled to stand there, had the charm of a child and the likeness of one of God's angels.

**Former Secret Service agent Clint Hill was
kind to sign this for my mom.**

**In October 2013, my mom went to pick this up at the
Partyville store right around the corner. Both copies I later found
on the seat after she suffered a massive stroke.**

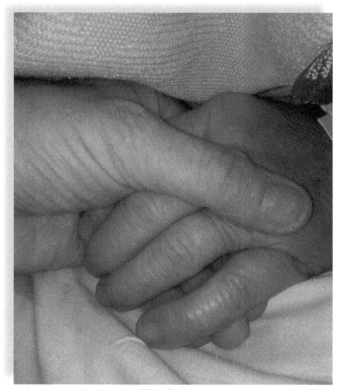

As my mother lay in a Toledo hospital, I held her hand
as she slipped away to heaven, as a tear fell from her eye.

The Kennedy Experience logo

CHAPTER 21

MY FRANCHISE HISTORY

I worked for McDonald's from the 9th grade until I graduated high school. I stayed in the business until I was 42 years old. You see, I am not a quitter. I stay the course and never give up on what I believe in. That conviction does not always prove to be the right path, but it's the one I've taken in life.

All during high school, my classmates called me Ronald McDonald. That was annoying, but the job taught me a lot. Over the years, I owned multiple McDonald's franchises.

But when I was 23, I purchased a Domino's Pizza franchise.

In 1977, a friend of mine and his wife visited us. Chuck lived a few blocks away from me when we were kids, so we'd grown up together. We were best friends as kids, and now we were both married with small children of our own.

When Chuck told us about a new restaurant that had just opened, we decided to check it out. So we ordered a pizza and went to pick it up for our wives.

As soon as we arrived at the brand new Domino's Pizza store, I was impressed. Everything was uniform, color-coded, and neat, from the workers uniforms and the delivery vehicles to the napkins and the pizza boxes. My career at McDonald's had taught me how to recognize a business with special attributes. The kind that marked a company for success.

I asked the store owner about Domino's: where was the company located, who were the owners, and were they selling franchises? Mike Kraus answered all of my questions. He gave me the telephone number for the company headquarters and the names of the two people to speak to: Jerry Collassa, in charge of franchising, and Mr. Thomas S. Monaghan, founder and president of Domino's Pizza, Inc.

After Chuck and I got back to my house and the four of us ate that pizza, I couldn't wait to call Domino's in Ann Arbor. The pizza was delicious, and we could tell the ingredients were of the best quality.

On a warm June day, I was scheduled to meet the founder of Domino's Pizza. It is highly unlikely today that if you applied for a major franchise you would be asked to sit down with the creator, but Mr. Monaghan ran his company with his own set of standards. One was to interview prospective franchisees. I would learn much more about Mr. Monaghan over the next 20 years, and he is one of the people in my life I've admired the most.

My wife accompanied me on the drive to Ypsilanti. I'd needed to come up with a big chunk of cash in order to apply for a buy in, and my father had helped. I had not revealed that in my application, so I was hoping it wouldn't come up.

My wife and I were surprised when we arrived at Domino's Pizza headquarters. The building was a rather run down older facility with lots of clutter lying around, like pizza equipment and file boxes. We were ushered into Mr. Monaghan's simple style office, and we sat down with him.

Mr. Monaghan spoke of his five children and the fact that he had been an orphan raised by nuns. His faith in God was a central priority in his life, and he spoke of that freely. It was quite a story to hear, a rags to riches tale just like Ray Kroc's, the McDonald's founder who grew up poor in Chicago. Tom Monaghan had a genuine sincerity and a palpable sense of gratitude. He was appreciative of what life had given him.

To my surprise, Mr. Monaghan asked me about my hobbies. When I explained that I collected presidential history memorabilia, specifically President Kennedy items. He seemed quite interested. He asked a lot of questions, which I found strange until I learned the reason for it. I almost fell off my chair when Mr. Monaghan told us that when he served in the US Marines, he bunked with Lee Harvey Oswald! Life does have some unusual twists and turns; this was one of them for me.

He suddenly said, "How does a young man such as yourself acquire so much cash?"

I was nervous, but I explained that the money and bank accounts were my father's. My dad had the same name as me, and he had allowed me to use his for the purpose of getting a foot in the door at Domino's. I went on to assure Mr. Monaghan that, if approved, I would do whatever was necessary to become a successful franchisee. I said that with my management background at McDonald's, I would be a good addition to the company, and I promised him I would not let him down.

"You won't regret this," I said. And I meant it.

He looked directly at me and said, "So you lied."

I said, "No. I am telling you now before we begin so that you are aware of the situation. I hope you are aware of my good intentions."

He said, "Yes, I am."

Mr. Collassa walked by the office and Mr. Monaghan motioned him in. "Jerry, would it be a problem if we co-signed a note for Fred at a bank? Will there be any problem if we do that?"

Mr. Collassa was the vice president and comptroller. He said, "No, not at all."

So that was it. Domino's would sign the $30,000 bank note with the First National Bank of Monroe.

It was done and I had my first franchise.

Later on I found out there was another reason for Mr. Monaghan's interest in my JFK collection. He also collected. Due to his admiration for Frank Lloyd Wright, Mr. Monaghan had quite a collection of the famous architect belongings. He dreamed of someday building one of Wright's designs for the Domino's Pizza world headquarters. He accomplished that years later when he built a magnificent building in Ann Arbor using Wright's grand design. Much later, Mr. Monaghan's dream sparked an idea of my own when I decided to build a White House museum to house my Kennedy Presidential collection.

I trained, then opened a franchise in Dearborn. It was a demanding project, and I was missing out on quality time with my growing family. I worked 10- to 14-hour days, and came home exhausted. But I loved the work.

One day I had an idea for my new Domino's. I remembered seeing Mr. Monaghan's Silver Shadow parked at the headquarters. I called him to make a proposal: I wanted to use his Rolls Royce for two weeks in order to deliver the country's finest pizzas in one of the world's finest automobiles. I said I would hire a chauffeur in uniform to open the door for the delivery person.

Tom Monaghan loved the idea. So I picked up his Silver Shadow Rolls. Then I called the local newspaper in Dearborn to tell them about the program, and they ran an article with a photo of Tom's Rolls. I did not say whose car it was and no one asked.

We did not promise a Domino's Rolls Royce Delivery for every order, but our phones rang off the hook after the article hit. And one thing was for sure, everyone knew the new Domino's was open!

As Domino's Pizza grew into a massive enterprise, I was proud to be part of something so big. I was also proud to help Mr. Monaghan in every way I could. Yes, he signed my bank note, but the loyalty was not about the money. My loyalty was to that good man at the top.

In early 1980, I took a few moments away from my Domino's store and drove to the nearby McDonald's in Dearborn Heights. When I walked in, the owner was there. I was at Rich's store often to pick up lunch or dinner for my crew, so we were friends.

Rich informed me that McDonald's had just opened the list for new franchisees. The list had been closed because there were enough people in training to buy all the available stores. Now they were opening more locations and needed buyers.

It didn't take long for that light to go off in my head. If I wanted to buy a McDonald's, now was the time

I sent for an application. Right away I ran into the usual obstacle: money. I owned a home in Michigan and my pizza franchise. But I was cash strapped because we had three young children ages 6, 4, and 3. The mortgage on my home was $235 a month, and I still owed nearly $30,000 on the Domino's bank note. I had virtually no money in the bank. Domino's was a struggling franchise at that time; most of the stores were located on college campuses or near a military base. I did not have a winning location. There were a dozen other pizza places within my delivery area. My sales averaged $3000 a week.

It was very difficult to put food on the table in those days, but in many ways I was never happier living a simple life.

I knew I had to convince McDonald's that they needed me. I'd been with them for so many years. And I had played a role in some of their special moments.

When I was 17, I met the founder of the company Ray Kroc. I was in Oakbrook, Illinois, attending Hamburger University. McDonald's headquarters was in a beautiful white building and Ray's office was located on the top floor. I introduced myself and told him which store I worked in. Ray knew the sales there, and he ran the numbers for me. His reputation for recall was totally accurate. He was an amazing man, a visionary, very aggressive as a businessman but very generous as a person. Another man I have admired for my entire adult life.

I really wanted to have my own franchise, but I was not going to put my father's bank account numbers on the application this time. There had to be a better way for my application to stand out from the thousands of others the company would receive.

I decided to take the honest route. I filled out the application indicating I had a home worth $58,000 with a $26,000 mortgage, 3 kids, a Domino's Pizza franchise, and not much cash. I sent a cover letter listing my long years of experience at McDonald's. I included my role in one of their industrial films.

In 1971, we had a field consultant named Larry Zimmerman. He would come by the store to conduct quality checks and make sure that the McDonald's standards were being met. I was told afterward that he spotted me working the counter and was impressed with my level of enthusiasm and good attitude. I'd had no idea I was being watched.

As it turned out, McDonald's was looking for a crew member from each region (there were 6) for a film. They chose me, and I was flown to Oakbrook, Illinois, to make the film.

I was so excited! I was still a kid, and my parents were so proud of me.

The film was a big success. It was shown at the World Wide Owner Operator Convention in Hawaii later that year. There I was on the big screen, according to my boss who attended. In the film, we discussed what it was like working at McDonald's and what kind of problems we encountered. I said, "They give you a shirt and tie, tell you to go do your job, then yell at you for not doing your job correctly. They just throw you in there."

I shook hands with the founder of McDonald's when I was in his office as a teenager. I would shake his hand again as a 26-year-old franchisee of the McDonald's Corporation. After that, I would attend the conventions myself, traveling to far-flung locations.

But first I had to resolve the money problem. In order to buy a franchise, I had to sell my Domino's Pizza franchise.

At the interview, I was asked why I would want to sell a franchise I had worked so hard to build. Unprepared, my answer came from deep inside: "McDonald's was not only my first real job, but my first love." I meant every word and the interviewers knew it.

McDonald's had many kinds of applicants, lots of people wanted to own a store. They told me there were plenty of rich people they could sell franchises to, and they got applications every day from them. But wealthy people had little incentive to work hard, and owning a McDonald's required that kind of self-determination. They looked at me and said, "We have nothing to lose with you because you know what hard work is and you want to be successful."

I reread my Domino's Pizza franchise agreement. There was a buy-out agreement (there are no buyout agreements today) that stated Domino's would buy my store based on a formulated price to calculate the trailing 12 months' net sales. The amount came to $29,998.98 as of March, 1980. I only needed $15,000 for the security deposit for a McDonald's store.

On April 1, 1980, I sold my Domino's Pizza store in Dearborn. Doug Dawson, Domino's financial VP, handed me a check for $29,998.98, all bank debts paid in full. He also informed me that Tom Monaghan wished me well, and if I ever wanted to return to Domino's I would be welcomed back.

I trained at Rich's store. It would take six months to own my own store, but there was plenty to do. I took classes, and found a location that my family liked. We sold the house in Michigan and moved to sunny Florida.

The very first week I owned the McDonald's in Fort Lauderdale, the windows and ceilings were shot up with a machine gun. This was retaliation from the strip club next door. The owners had asked to use my parking lot at night after we were closed. I said no, and we kept the entrance and exit chained up. The bar owners offered me $1000. When I said no, they offered me $500. Then I was told they were going to use my lot and not pay for the opportunity.

I did not want the broken beer bottles, horseplay by drunks, and possible damage to the building, so I kept saying no. They did not like that.

I had just arrived home from work after an 18-hour day when the assistant manager called to tell me what happened. Janice was young, and had been working at the location before I purchased it. She was in tears when I asked my first question. "Was anyone shot?"

No one was shot, but the employees were understandably upset and scared. I told her to wait for the police and I would call a board-up service. I told her to send everyone home. She could lock up, and I would take care of everything in the morning.

I was working in the new restaurant for 12 to15 hours a day and I lived a long drive west. So at that time, I thought it was the right thing to do. Now I would drive right back to the store and stay there all night, but I was still young and a bit naïve.

I had become even more of a workaholic than when I owned the Domino's store. My wife was complaining that I was never home, and she was correct. People who have great career opportunities like I had see the light at the end of the tunnel. We generally do not see the tunnel we are actually in. That figurative tunnel may be more money or a new house to others. In my case, that light was the goal of making my store run smoothly and making it profitable. Once that was accomplished, I would not have to be there all the time.

I got up the next morning at 4 and drove to the store. There was a lot of glass all over the lot and many boarded-up windows. What a depressing sight. But I pulled out my positive attitude and went to work. First I cleaned up the floors and threw away the food that had been left out when I sent everyone home. I counted the cash from the previous night. And I opened at 7 a.m.

An hour later, an elderly employee walked over while I was working the front counter. Mildred had worked for the previous owner. She was a graceful grandmother who made the store a better place to be. People loved her.

She said she was sorry but she did not feel well and asked if she could leave. Her face looked pale. I told her not to worry, she should go home and rest. Poor Mildred looked at me and smiled, turned away, took a few steps, and slipped to the floor.

Crack! She hit her head when she landed on the hard tile.

Mildred died that day, right there in the store. By the time the ambulance came, it was too late.

Two days later, the hearse stopped for a moment in front of my McDonald's as a symbolic gesture of farewell to the crew. Everyone was crying. This moment is still vivid in my mind and I think of it often.

Over the next 13 years, the business was robbed 6 times and I was robbed at my home twice. The final robbery at McDonald's was on my 18th wedding anniversary, ruining the day for my wife and I. We were on the skids by that time so it was not what we needed.

I should have listened to Gary.

Gary Smith was my McDonald's field consultant at the time. He later became an owner/operator, and my best friend. One day during the early months of my store, Gary came by. He asked me to step outside. It was another beautiful South Florida day. We sat down at one of the round patio tables under an umbrella next to a tall palm tree with big green fronds.

Gary and I were products of the baby boom generation, so "making it" was part of the culture while we were growing up. Many fathers (including mine) encouraged their sons to go out and make some real money, create a business, buy a home, and start a family. Like many in my generation, I believed this was the American dream.

But Gary had watched me spend 14-hour days in my restaurant—day after day after day. So he figured he would give me some advice, wisdom he'd accrued from his own life experiences.

As we sat there in the shade of the iconic palm tree, my friend looked at me and said, "Listen, guy, you need to remember to spend some quality time with your family. Don't burn yourself out.

Go home early some days, take your wife and kids to the park for a few hour. Do something, anything, to be sure you make time for them. It's important."

I nodded. This was what my wife had been saying, and I knew both of them were right.

Gary said, "Look at that palm tree. That tree will be there today, tomorrow, and next year, and it was there before you got here. But your family will only be there, the way they are right now, one time in your life. I've seen families blow up because somebody isn't around. Don't make that mistake! Please don't go down that road. The tree will still be there!"

Ray Kroc used to say that a businessman can go home and complain about what he did all day, or he can come home and brag about what he did at work, then go out and paint the town red with his spouse. He knew how to make a marriage work.

What I failed to realize until it was too late, well into my marriage and well after my children were in their teens, was this: my good natured attitude at home allowed me to be taken advantage of. No one's perfect, and I certainly made my share of mistakes. I was guilty of spending many, many hours at work. But I had a big family to support in an expensive part of the country, so I wasn't away from home because I was a bad husband and father. I was trying my best to provide for my family by making my business a success.

It takes two to make a marriage work, but only one to destroy it. I was caught in a success trap that would eventually doom my marriage. And lead to the worst time of my life.

Despite the inauspicious start, my business took off. Net sales volume over the next ten years at my store went from $599,000 dollars a year to a whopping $1.42 million. Profits grew to levels that amazed me with an unbelievable 120 months of consecutive monthly increases. The McDonald's company awarded me for that with a rare commendation.

But my family came first and we needed to make some changes. The tree would always be there.

Finally, we made the decision to move away from South Florida. We hoped our marriage and our kids' lives would improve.

Unfortunately, the grass is not greener on the other side. I learned that soon after arriving in South Carolina.

Graduation, May 1972. By 1977, I owned Domino's Pizza, then became the youngest owner/ operator franchisee of McDonald's Corporation at 26 years old on September 15, 1980.

**At 23 pictured here helping out the construction of
my first franchise on Telegraph Road, Dearborn, Michigan, 1977**

Domino's Pizza logo in 1977.
Domino's dropped the "Pizza."
Its signs now say "Domino's."
McDonald's dropped the
Hamburglar from logos and
road signs long ago.

On the makeline 1977–78

Thomas S. Monaghan,
founder Domino's Pizza, Inc.

Domino's farms and office complex built in 1985 in
Frank Lloyd Wright–inspired prairie school style.
Set to blend seamlessly into a serene, natural setting.

I chronicled my entire life in photos not realizing it until I wrote this book.
Pictured here is Executive CFO Jerry Kolassa congratulating me and
giving some support to sales in October 1977!

Working fifteen hours as day, on my way to success as planned

Mr. Monaghan came in to see and discuss my sales as I was one of the first
locations that was in a rural American neighborhood—
most were located on military bases and college campuses.

Using a seven-foot clown and free Coca-Cola, McDonald's marketing taught me to do something different and first.

1977–1980 School Student tour making their own pizzas. Dearborn Michigan. I brought over school tours as we did at our McDonalds Restaurants.

He loved the idea but said to me, "You're kidding, right?" when I said I wanted to borrow his Rolls to deliver the finest pizza in one of the finest automobiles.

Cool pizza uniforms with industry-used paper hats as we also spun each dough ball!

In April 1972, my owner/operator Bernie Schmitt sent me to Chicago to Hamburger University. This was my senior year spring break. When I came back, I was promoted to one of his general managers in Monroe, Michigan.

At age 24 (above) with Domino's Pizza car and my blue Chevy wagon I left at Domino's headquarters when I picked up Mr. Monaghan's Rolls, 1977

In 1972 Fred Turner (above), Ray Kroc's right-hand man who became president and CEO of McDonald's over time. He began as a crew member on the grill. Ray noticed he was excellent, and they grew the McDonald's system to the number-one franchise in the world.

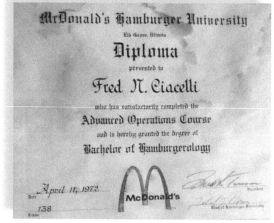

Yes, there is a Hamburger University! Unknowingly I would return in August 1980 at 26 years old to Chicago as a registered applicant and then become an owner/operator by September 15, 1980.

I took photos at almost every special time in my life. This was the new HU. My class was #138 in April 1980. More than five thousand students attend Hamburger University each year, and over two hundred seventy-five thousand people have graduated with a degree in "Hamburgerology."

April 1972 in Chicago, Illinois. I would become an owner in a short eight years in 1980.

With McDonald's Corporation "vice president of individuality" Jim Kuhn and six outstanding crew members from the six company regions. Title: "What's it like working at McDonald's?"

With Founder of McDonald's Ray A. Kroc at San Francisco owner operator convention. I said, "I have unit #2011 in Fort Lauderdale." He took my arm and said, "Oh, I've seen your progress. I know that store well—your increase in sales is fantastic! I see we have the right person for the job."

Ray died on January 14, 1984. I put my flag at half-staff. A McDonald's executive called and asked why. I said, "Ray died today." Not sure they appreciated that, but I kept in that way the entire weekend.

The flagship all-American meal, 1972. Hamburger 28 cents, French Fries 26 cents, Triple Thick Shake 35 cents. 89 cents total before tax—you got change back from your dollar!

This is the dining room as I took over a losing location of
sales below $600,000.00 and turning a loss.

If you own a McDonald's, there is constant spending of large sums of capital
on dining rooms, outside appearance, new equipment, lighting, signage, crew
uniforms, and the list is long. You do not argue when it is suggested you make
some changes. Here, all new seating, walls, ceiling, and more.

I matched new blue tile with behind-the-counter accents along with
blue menu inserts. If you're an owner, you spend money. It's just what you do
if you want to succeed and get offered additional locations.

Just a few years earlier, there I am at a groundbreaking with my owners Bernie
and Donna Schmitt (pictured in center holding spatula).

Unit #2011. After I took over, I removed the
tables from the front, installed new ones, and
added a wood structure playland in the early
1980s. In 1993 came another investment of
nearly $400,000 with a far upgraded play
structure and another remodel.

In 1993, a $400K full store remodel—dining, roof, floors, restrooms, new AC
units, added office, added double-booth drive-through, clam grills, fryers,
ceilings, vents, new large playland, seating, TV, and decor. We used a 1960s
theme and used only black, white, and grey interior and red menu boards.

New double-booth drive-through with my design office in the center.
Washing guests' windshields as they say hello to Mac tonight.

A proud mom and dad in 1993-1994 Fort Lauderdale in new complete
store remodel. Other locations I've owned were also remodeled
shortly after I purchased them. McDonald's operators were
required to consistently reinvent in their stores.

Smartest field consultant and my best friend
pictured here at JFK show in Novi, Michigan, 2013.
The world lost this brilliant man of advice on February 23, 2019.

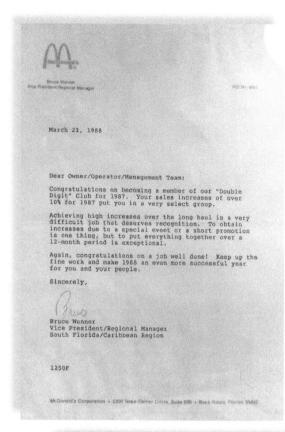

Letter from Vice President Bruce Wunner. The store continued to show sales increases for the entire fourteen years. I babied the hell out of that location with unusual marketing and promotion ideas. The secret to all this is one more ingredient: hire, explain, and drill it into their heads what a positive attitude *actually is*. Then expect and look for it every shift.

In 1981 with Mike Potter (manager), Mike Polley, Debbie Moore, Laurie L., Tim Keating, Jamie Kennedy, and others. Since I began as a crew member at the age of fifteen, I understood the downsides to the work and made things fun and enjoyable and rewarded them all year with more than just a paycheck.

CHAPTER 22

JFK: JAILED FOR KENNEDY

It was a warm summer day in July of 1998 and I had just returned from a concert in West Palm Beach, Florida. At my house at Deerfield Beach, there was a frantic pounding on the front door. I opened it to two Broward County Sheriff deputies in riot gear. They said they wanted to ask me some questions.

What the heck?

A SWAT team officer informed me they had a warrant for my arrest. He showed it to me, and asked if the person in it was my ex-wife.

It wasn't. The warrant was due to a harassment claim. A false claim made by my own daughter!

The warrant was for a telephone harassment charge out of South Carolina. This was a legal maneuver used to get me to that state.

As part of our divorce settlement, my wife wanted the Kennedy collection. I refused to hand over my life's work. She had no interest in JFK, and had made that clear to me for years. This was my passion and all she would do was sell it off.

Our disagreement on this was a civil matter so I was not legally required to go to South Carolina. But I didn't know that.

My ex's attorney was a clever lawyer. She had created a criminal charge in order to lure me back to the state. I later filed a complaint against her with the South Carolina lawyers oversight board. The other attorneys resigned from the case because they knew this was

173

against my civil rights. I was being arrested for telephone harassment in the state of South Carolina while living in South Florida.

I was in shock to see that I was accused of threatening my daughter over the telephone, which of course never happened. I loved my daughter and called her every week to chat. But she had been persuaded to make a false statement. This was later revealed in court. My 20-year-old daughter had been convinced by my wife's attorney that she could help her mother by lying about me.

As I stood there with the cops in all their gear, I was sweating. I was confused. I didn't know my rights. The SWAT officer said the warrant was not something we had here in Broward County. He said their officers would call the accused and tell them to stop the phone harassment, and they would never make an arrest over such a thing with no proof of guilt. He had to take me in, he said, but he thought I'd be out of jail and home by the next day.

It's been almost a year and I'm still in jail.

They drove me to the station and I was booked into the Broward County jail. I spent over a month there while they figured out what to do about the contempt charge in South Carolina. The judge had made the charge after I refused to hand over my JFK collection. Since there was a bond on the phone charge but there was no bond on the contempt of court, I was held for the South Carolina civil charge.

First of all, let me say that going to jail can happen to anyone. People go to jail for many reasons. One does not have to be an actual criminal to go to jail for such violations as driving with no license or tags, missing child support payments, mistaken identity, and a range of minor offences.

Let me also explain that there are different reasons for being accused of contempt of court. If a person is belligerent to the judge in a courtroom or uses profanity, that can lead to a contempt charge. Another form of contempt of court is failure to comply with a court order.

What court order did *I* not comply with? I was ordered by a judge to give my ex-wife my entire Kennedy collection including the 1961 replica car. At the time, my collection included over 10,000 items. When I refused, Judge Georgia V. Anderson of Spartanburg, South Carolina, gave me a one year sentence for contempt of court. Attorney Grace Dunbar, now Grace Gilcrest Knie, was ruthless in attacking me, leaving me in jail for the contempt charge and the second false charge—which was later dismissed.

So here I am, in jail, writing this book.

Entrance to the center (left). I nearly ran out that hellhole when they called my name at 5:30 a.m., "Ciacelli, JFK PACK IT UP."

Typical floor plan (right). There are *no* jail bars—normal doors with a small window. Normally there are two inmates; however, a third one may sleep on a cot when overcrowding occurs.

This is the humiliating condition of sleeping quarters (left): bunk bed with aluminum toilet with no seat, aluminum sink, and polished metal that is supposed to be a mirror.

CHAPTER 23

MAKING THE MOST OF JAIL

So I have been incarcerated in the county jail in Spartanburg, South Carolina, for contempt of court for refusing to abide by a court order. An order to give up my life's work to someone who didn't deserve it or appreciate it.

I preferred jail.

The legal system was not friendly to someone like me. I learned to deal with this reality as time went on. A judge's fiduciary duty is to set an equitable division of assets. This was not the case. When I asked the judge, is this fair to me, she replied, "Who said I have to be fair?"

The moment she said that, I was filled with renewed energy. My spirit lifted and I realized I would do whatever it took to keep my collection from my ex. If I had to go to jail, so be it. I would never give my ex-wife the collection I had built to share with the world.

So I was ordered to spend a year in jail. Even though I had committed no crime. This does something to you deep inside your soul. Believe me, it's an experience you would not want to have. Here I was, locked up in jail with real criminals—people who had killed, burned down businesses, stolen cars, robbed and beaten others. I shared space with drug dealers, crazy people, and one kid who had a threatened Chelsea Clinton, the president's daughter.

It was so crowded that I slept on the floor for a month before a cell was freed up. It's cold all the time here, and food is on your mind constantly. Never getting to see the clouds or green grass, birds or trees, takes a toll on you. You get no privacy. Whether you are using the bathroom, showering, brushing your teeth, or sleeping, there is always someone in your space. County jail is not federal prison. It's rough. You're uncomfortable, scared, bored, and trapped inside with some dangerous characters—and you kinda go a little crazy.

On Christmas day, I went to the local canteen. With my hands folded behind my back, I was standing in line, waiting to be called up to the window. At the commissary you can buy items like snacks, soda, bubblegum, honey buns, cigarettes, socks, and other stuff—but only if you have the money. A friend of mine who owned a local McDonald's sends me $100 a month from my bank account. That way, I can at least enjoy a few little extras. Another owner/operator, Don Pollock, and his wife Audrey, sent me a six-month subscription to *USA Today*. They told me in a letter that they wanted me to see what's going on in the outside world. Their kindness really helped boost my mood.

Normally I would just purchase a soda and chips. But since it was Christmas, I felt compelled to give something to someone else instead.

I asked the canteen attendant how many items I was allowed to buy. He said ten of each item, but that was it. So I spent the entire $100 on ten packs of cigarettes, ten honey buns, ten cans of soda, ten candy bars, ten bags of chips, ten pairs of socks, ten cans of small pre-cooked hotdogs, ten bags of M&Ms, and whatever else I could afford.

When I got back to my pod, I asked the guard if I could cover one table with newspaper and set up a Christmas buffet of sorts.

By now my name was no longer Fred, they all called me JFK. He said, sure, JFK, go for it.

After the guard gave me permission, I began placing the items in rows until the table was completely full. I arranged the items in a pile that looked like a volcano. I had opened a 10-pack of cigarettes and lined up each one end to end, all around the table in a circle. When I finished I made this announcement: *Fellow criminals, who are of course innocent, merry Christmas from me! Come enjoy yourselves!*

My jail mates stood there staring at me and the table. Finally, they got the message and swarmed that table like a bunch of locusts. In only a few minutes, the stainless steel table was empty. Not even a single potato chip or lifesaver was left.

I was watching TV in the main room when a group of inmates approached me. They said it was a good thing I did for them for Christmas. They told me thank you.

I didn't plan to do this in the days leading up to the holiday, but like most ideas that hit you at no special moment, this was one of my best. It was especially rewarding because it made me feel like a normal human being.

Jail was a miserable place for me to be. My attorney described me as a man out of his element. This was so true. However, a man's personality is impossible to change in any circumstance. So I tried to make the best of it because I figured the time had to pass eventually, then I would be free.

For a long time, I was missing my new husky malamute, the mixed breed I named Honey. She had ice blue eyes and soft blond fur, that dog was like a dream. I got her when she was just nine weeks old, right before I left for South Carolina. Whenever I cried during the early months in county jail, it was because I was thinking about her or looking at her photo. I was reduced to a crybaby not knowing when I would see my dog again.

Writing this book only filled so much of the deep void in my life. I was hungry almost all the time because the meals were based on the cheap, institutional, horrible diet the State dictated. I like my food. My mother was an excellent cook, and I was around food all the time as a franchise owner. So I knew my way around food, and the crap they served was not food. I wanted more food to eat, and good food, not the tasteless meals and canteen snacks.

So I devised a plan.

Since most of the inmates had no money to go to the canteen, I began to purchase cigarettes every day. These would be for the smokers who were going through withdrawal. I observed them picking cigarette butts off the floor or going through the ashtrays just to get a drag or two of nicotine. So the idea of food for smokes seemed plausible.

I would swap two or three cigarettes with the addicts for a breakfast, lunch, or dinner. This was in no way a straight up deal. Inmates are not allowed to change seats in the meal room or give food to others, and you can't trade for food. If you are caught making any of these violations, you go into lockdown for a week—or longer. This means you have to stay in your cell 24/7, except for a five-minute shower once daily. No TV in the main rooms, no reading material, no phone use, and no visit to the canteen to buy snacks. Intolerable.

Most guards spoke to us like we were garbage. Profanity was yelled at us, and we were always being threatened with isolation. This happened every single shift. Most of the guards have mental problems, they seem like sociopaths to me.

My cigarettes for meals plan worked for a while; I had enough to eat, but the food was still crappy.

Then things got turned around. Some of the smokers wanted more cigarettes, and fights broke out. This was a big deal. Alarms went off, sirens and flashing lights, and the uniformed SWAT style commandos arrived to surround the pod.

This was scary. The experience made me feel like a real criminal. I kept repeating, *This is only a movie, right? This is only a movie, this is not real.* The mantra helped calm me down until the Army guys left.

One time when I was at lunch, a fight broke out at my table. We were all instructed to go immediately to our cells. I got up and walked up the stainless steel stairs, went down the hall to my cell and lay down on my bunk. A couple of days later, we were all still in confinement. A guard came into my cell. He wanted me to sign a statement. The State wanted to put additional charges on one of the inmates, so the statement indicated that he had initiated the fight.

The powers that be were not happy with my refusal to sign the statement. Most of the guards hated this particular inmate. But he was not to blame.

The guards are deliberate narcissists and love having power over others. If I had a video of what they said to us most of the time, it would make your skin crawl. The facility is clean, but the guards make it intolerable. Some of the inmates are bothersome as well.

For example, one young black kid with a gold grill saw me reading issues of *Time* and *Newsweek* a friend had sent me. He told me he wanted the magazines when I was done. We are not allowed to share reading material, so if the issues were found in another cell, all my mail would be stopped and no more reading material would be allowed. I couldn't bear that.

When I told him that, he did not care. The kid just wanted the staples from the magazines to use as a needle.

A few days later, he walked by my cell, poked his head in, and said, "I'm going to get you, motherfucker!"

Now I had a problem. I was facing threats. I'd learned earlier in my life that, when threatened with adversity, most people tend to think of a solution rather than react to the situation at hand. I didn't have many options as we were all locked up in the same enclosed area. I could not even think of a way to get around the threat.

However, an idea popped into my mind in one of those odd moments. I saw that he was waiting for me and I blurted, "Look, I will give you the magazines if you can beat me at chess. One game, that's it. But if I beat you, then it's over. You leave me alone."

To my surprise, he said okay, let's do it.

The next day, we sat down at a steel table and began our game of chess. In six moves, I said checkmate.

I must say, the kid is a man of his word. From that day on, he became my friend. He asked me to explain how the stock market works and how to start a business. But we lost touch when I was transferred to another pod.

In my new pod, I learned that if you become a trustee you get certain privileges because you are helping to run the pod. Trustees clean the showers, sweep the floors, and keep the place clean. In exchange, you can keep your door open all day—which is an amazing feeling when you've been locked up like a caged beast for months. And best of all, time is taken off your sentence, moving up a release date by two days for every 30 worked as a trustee.

I had already made up my mind to sign on when I discovered that the trustees were given extra food. In exchange for pouring drinks and handing out food trays three times a day, trustees were given extra food and drink at every meal worked. This meant I could leave behind my cigarettes for food project and work the system another way.

With my background in restaurants, I knew I could be extra helpful. And gain access to more, and possibly better, food.

I talked to one of the guards. I told him about my restaurants, and asked him put me in charge of serving the food since I could coordinate the workers. I said we needed more time to eat after finishing the kitchen work. The work was so inefficient that it took almost the whole meal hour and the workers were left with only five minutes to eat. With more efficient mealtimes, the trustees would have additional time for our own meals.

This particular guard was not one of the sociopaths and he said sure, let's do it.

There were three other trustees helping at each meal. I told them this: you pour the ice, you pour the sweet tea, you hand out the tray. When one of them asked so what do you do, I said, "I watch you to make sure you do it right."

The three of them laughed.

I was serious. I said, "Listen, men, if you can stay focused we will get all the food we want three times a day. Just listen to me and do what I ask you to do."

They agreed, and we served a meal my way.

To their surprise but not mine, instead of taking the usual 55 minutes to feed the pod, we were finished in about 35. This gave the trustees a whopping 25 minutes to eat as much food as we wanted.

We continued in this manner, which allowed us to dine well at breakfast, lunch, and dinner. So much for going hungry.

Large plate glass windows from floor to ceiling separated a section of the pod. I asked the rational guard why the windows were never cleaned. He said he did not think about it. I told him, "So why don't you have someone get me the supplies to clean them? If I give you a list and you get me the supplies, I'll get these windows clean for you."

The guard said, "You got to be kidding, right?"

I said, "I'm in jail, do I look like I'm kidding? I'm in this hellhole and I'm bored and I need something constructive to do."

A few days later, the guard brought me the cleaning supplies: a squeegee, an extended stick, a ladder, window cleaner, and fresh dry towels. I soaked the windows down good, brushed them, then used the squeegee. I dried the best I could with newsprint and the towels.

Some of the other guards came over to see what I'd done. Somebody said, "We can't let JFK leave here. These windows never looked so good!"

Ha ha.

A female guard took an interest in me after this. She was very nice to me, and began to chat with me during the night shift. She would watch me, and come sit next to me in the main room. She was smart. I didn't mind talking to someone other than criminals and our conversations were a breath of fresh air. As the weeks went by, we shared a lot of about our lives. She knew the stupid reason why was in jail, and she was angry about that. She told me about how the Spartanburg County judicial system really worked. Normally a divorce case contempt of court earned you a week in jail, not a year.

The guard knew about Judge Anderson and Attorney Dunbar, and she said they'd probably worked together to keep me in jail for a year. They had figured nobody would sit out that kind of punishment, and they were sure I'd give in. I found this kind of insight to be both enlightening and depressing.

When I got out, I sent complaints to the South Carolina Bar Association regarding the attorney for overreach, fake trumped-up charge of a misdemeanor and conspiracy for gain on a civil suit. I volunteered to go to South Carolina from Florida and the charge was dropped. Those who made that report were told what they did could cause themselves a charge for making a false report. I actually heard this with my own ears from the County Solicitor as the door was wide open near as I sat close to the door. I was served while in chains the formal contempt charge for refusing to give up 100% of my Kennedy Collection.

Now attorney turned Judge Grace Gilchrist Dunbar Knie in her application to become a Judge answered questions regarding if there were any such complaints, accusations, or ethical past history. I believe she either lied, had a poor memory or misspoke about what her version was in the case. She even had the charge incorrectly stated on the application to give her possible additional credibility.

Fellow McDonald's owner Gary Smith sent me this original photo of Honey. I looked at it every day, but it made me even more sad. It's still in my wallet today. When she died at the age of sixteen in 2013, there was no way I could survive without having a dog to love. Annie arrived in 2013. Sadly at only nine years old and with no notice, out of the blue, she suffered several brain seizures in the early morning hours of Sunday, October 23, 2022.

Honey inside the famous limo. Going down the road with the presidential limo and her inside got a lot of looks.

Annie, named after mom

My sweet girl, sadly missed

EPILOGUE

It was 5:30 in the morning. An announcement over the loudspeaker said, "Ciacelli, JFK, pack it up!"

That's the code for you can go home now. I was up and grabbing my stuff in seconds. I was getting the hell out of that hellhole!

I packed up my book, which was written in longhand on a couple dozen yellow legal pads. The guards came over to wish me good luck. They seemed less like sociopaths and more like okay people. I bid goodbye to the female guard, an actual friend, the trustees I'd worked the meals with, and some of my pod mates. Then I picked up my box of stuff and walked out. Forever.

It was April 16, 1999, and I was a free man again.

I walked out of the front of the Spartanburg County Detention Center. I took taxi to a postal center and mailed my box to my home in South Florida. Then I asked the driver to please take me to McDonald's so I could have a Big Mac, large fries, and a large Coke.

My American Express card was still good. I ate my first decent meal in months, then the driver took me to the airport and I bought a one-way ticket to Fort Lauderdale.

The woman behind the desk saw my jail tag on my left wrist. My hair was disheveled and I had that look of shock to be out in the world again. She said, "Would you like me to cut that off for you?"

I said yes and she did so. When she offered to me, I said, "Please throw it away. No one should ever see that again."

She laughed a little and said, "I bet."

A policeman standing near us said nothing.

On the flight home, a very large man sitting in the window seat. When I said hello, he turned his back on me.

The airline attendant walked by and asked if we would like something to drink. I asked for a cup of coffee. She also gave me a set of earbuds so I could listen to music.

I settled back and put on the earbuds. I was in heaven. My friend Gary was meeting me at the airport. I would see Honey again. I'd made it through the worst year in my life, and now I was above the clouds.

Elvis Presley's "I Did It MY way" came on. I could relate. As Elvis sang in his beautiful deep voice, I began to cry. My weeping was uncontrollable. I cried so hard I almost couldn't breathe, couldn't catch my breath. I couldn't stop and I was almost choking.

The flight attendant came over. She stroked y hair and told me that it was okay, everything would be all right. So kind. All I could say was, "I lost everything, I lost everything."

At the end of the flight, the man next to me said, "Hey, I'm really sorry the way I treated you. Please accept my apology." He also said he'd gone through a tough time in life himself. "I feel your pain. I am so sorry for the way I treated you. I had no idea you were in such peril."

This touched me. I said, "Thank you. It's okay."

When the flight landed, I met up with Gary. He drove us to Skyline Chili for my second great meal of the day. When we drove up to the house, I was surprised to see it had been decorated with "Welcome Home" signs. His four kids were there. Honey jumped up to greet me, licking me in her loving manner. I was happy she remembered me.

I had been keeping in touch with some of my Kennedy contacts while in jail. Melody Miller, the family spokesperson, called to say, "Catch your breath because John Kennedy wants to meet you. He wants to see the man who went to jail for a collection of his father's memorabilia. "She said Senator Ted Kennedy admired your moxie! I had to look up the word.

I was thrilled, but of course John Jr. died in a plane crash in July of that year, before we had a chance to meet. So tragic. I had planned to give him his dad's jewelry box.

During the first year I was home, two of the prison guards came to visit. To my surprise, they told me they were sorry about how unfairly I'd been treated by the justice system. I appreciated their honesty.

At this point, I had no McDonald's restaurant, no family, no car, a house and no cash. I knew it was time to reinvent myself.

To make some money, I worked several jobs: I ran the Ft. Lauderdale international Airport food division. I served brand manager for nine Dunkin' Donuts. I worked for other major corporations in a management capacity including Chick-fil-A, Taco Bell, Little Caesars, and Walgreens. I even opened a pizza place called Ciacelli's Presidential Pizza. The menu consisted of Ronald Reagan Balanced Budget Pizza, the Richard Nixon Two Term Pizza (which included two pizzas), Jackie Kennedy's Rose Garden salads, John-John junior hot dogs, and the Abe Lincoln Five Dollar Pizza Special. I served hot fresh popcorn while you waited for your pizza.

Eventually, I opened a flag company. My business is called the Flag Depot. I sell flags, install flagpoles, and will deliver the flags right to your house—just like a pizza. People love it.

The torture from my ex-wife and her attorney continued for eight years, as they pursued me for the collection. They threatened me with more jail time. Finally, they gave up.

When they did, I went back on the road with my JFK collection.

I traveled to 26 states with the exhibit. We appeared at casinos, home shows, home and garden shows, state fairs, and small local fairs. Over 1 million people have seen my JFK collection. I've been on numerous TV shows and have made a dozen movies about John F. Kennedy with the iconic 1961 Lincoln presidential limousine. After the ordeal in jail I did additional films, Stephen King's *11.22.63* (James Franco); Steven Spielberg's *All the Way* (HBO) (Brian Cranston); National Geographic's *The Lost Bullet*; Discovery Channel's *JFK, Inside the Target Car*; Warner Bros' *The Watchmen*; Speed Channel's *Behind the Headlights, The Kennedy Car*. Also, JFK Limo *Mysteries at the Museum, The Travel Channel*.

Look for me during the 60th anniversary year for President Kennedy's assassination. You might catch me at the exhibit in your town, or see me in the local newspaper or on TV. When you see me, I will be introduced as: *the man who went to jail for John F. Kennedy*.

My story includes numerous photos of the famous and not so famous, and offers readers a bitter sweet taste of history.

When I finally got home, I had to reinvent myself, find an income. I worked
on this book for years until finally completing it in late 2021.

Melody Miller, family spokesperson and office of
Senator Edward M. Kennedy pictured with the
president (left).

At Senator Kennedy's Washington, DC, office
with Melody Miller

Finally home. There's Honey. Gary and his family welcomed me back.

AUTHOR BIO

Fred Nicholas Ciacelli is an American entrepreneur where he began as a ten year-old selling cotton candy, lemonade and other things at the park from his wagon. His business ventures included becoming a franchisee at the ages of 23 and 26 years old. From a small town home of Gen. Custer in Monroe, Michigan he worked at a local hotdog stand then McDonald's restaurants starting at the age of 15. Later to own five McDonald's restaurants. With no cash in hand both Domino's & McDonald's financed him. He was told they saw in him something unique of his age, his drive, knowledge, passion, and most evident in his enthusiasm.

Mr. Ciacelli's life although has not been all together an easy one. He begins a JFK collection on the very day President Kennedy was shot and coming home from the fourth grade seeing his mother crying. After seeing his mother's sorrow he began a lifelong collection, buying everything related to the late President. His plan was to open a Museum then travel with it throughout the country keeping President Kennedy's memory alive through his world-class collection which he accomplished.

Mr. Ciacelli has been interviewed by hundreds of local and national news programs including, The Today Show. His custom-built 1961 Lincoln Continental duplicate limousine was built by the same company that built Kennedy's car. His iconic Limo has been in productions in 11 Hollywood and TV films. The Kennedy Experience Exhibition and the famous limousine enabled Mr. Ciacelli to meet Hollywood A-List movie stars, Presidents, Vice Presidents, Senators, even family members of JFK's. He also had his hair cut by the White House Salon barber Steve Martini when Mr. Martini retired in Boca Raton.

Rose Kennedy the President's mother and JFK's Brother, Edward M. Kennedy have written to him in regards to his wonderful dedication to the memory of the President.

Today Mr. Ciacelli when not on the road with the collection operates one of his entrepreneur companies called The Flag Depot. He resides in lighthouse Point Florida.

**My limo at Trump's Mara-Lago entrance
with Secret Service agent.**

With then-Senator Joe Biden. Washington, D.C.

Filming in South Florida (left) with ex-Department of Justice special JFK project, 2021

Former agent Clinton V. Hill (right) who climbed on the limo to save the president

Opening of JFK Experience with Kathleen Kennedy Townsend

Former Texas Governor John Connally

It's a hands-on job when you own a McDonald's and the billion number needs changing!

My story ran front page in the South Carolina city paper

My dad Fred retired from Ford Motor Company as a painter and was always there for me to spruce up the place.

JFK Remembered

3425 West Vine Street, Kissimmee 34741
Phone: (407) 932-1390

★ ★ ★ ★ ★ ★ ★ ★

Adults will remember.
Children will enjoy.

The museum experience the family will never forget.

Visit us and relive a time in our nation's history when things seemed a little simpler, life was a little better. The Kennedy years…

View the 1961 Presidential limousine
See original items from Air Force One
Videos from JFK's 1,000 days in office
Stand at the Presidential Podium
Memorabilia from the 1960 campaign
Compare your height to that of all
of the presidents.
Visit the Presidential newsroom

Admission Prices
Adult $6.00
Senior $5.00
Children under 12 free
Allow a 1-2 hour visit

Next to Fun-N-Wheels In The LaMirada Plaza

My Kennedy Museum rack card from Kissimmee, Florida (right)

★ ★ ★ ★ ★ ★ ★ ★

Open 7 days a week from 10:00 AM to 9:00 PM

Meeting Senator Edward Kennedy in Washington.

To Nick Ciacelli
4-28-2003
Always a pleasure to talk with you
S. Martini

A Lesson on Mature Men's Hair

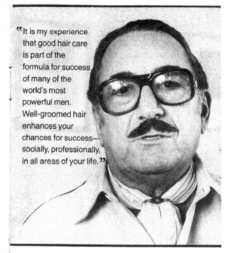

"It is my experience that good hair care is part of the formula for success of many of the world's most powerful men. Well-groomed hair enhances your chances for success— socially, professionally, in all areas of your life."

Steve Martini is one of America's foremost authorities on grooming for mature men. He was the official White House barber for Presidents Eisenhower, Kennedy, Johnson and Nixon.

Steve began his barbershop career at literally the bottom...shining shoes. Soon, he was giving haircuts, and after a few years opened a shop of his own.

World War II brought Steve to Washington, where he gave haircuts to many military men. By 1952, he was part of the official White House staff.

In his unique capacity as haircutter, Steve became a confidant to many powerful men. He came to know the Presidents, their advisors and their families. He and his wife, Ann, traveled and campaigned with them, relaxed with them and shared their joys and sorrows.

Today, Steve Martini is a consultant to the makers of GRECIAN® FORMULA 16,® a product that he says has changed his life. Steve and Ann own and operate the barbershop in Florida's Boca Raton Hotel. Life has changed for the Martini family from their days in the White House, as have men's grooming styles. He has found that many men, himself included, use GRECIAN® FORMULA 16® to get rid of gray.

Basically, all hair is made of strong, elastic, rope-like fibers of protein. These, in turn, are held together by softer protein particles which give the hair its lustre.

Each strand of hair contains *melanin*, which determines its color. Although the quality of melanin is the same in all hair, its quantity differs from strand to strand, creating, on any given head, shades of brown or black, etc., rather than one, uniform color.

HAIR CROSS SECTION

As most people age, the production of melanin diminishes, sooner in some hairs than in others. The hair continues to grow, only without as much pigmentation. The less melanin, the grayer the hair. When no melanin is produced, the hair is white.

Also, with age, oil secretions can decrease, leaving hair brittle, dry and more vulnerable to damage. These are some of the reasons why the hair of mature men demands special treatment.

I got a few haircuts from Kennedy's own White House barber, Steve Martini. Boca Raton, Florida

Ronald and both Kennedy limos were used in local promotions.

TV interview with Extra TV that went national.
Deerfield Beach, Florida
https://www.youtube.com/watch?v=Ru5lyG9l1No

Owning this opened many doors and opportunities.

Kissimmee JFK Remembered 1990

My iconic reproduction at Space Garden, Kennedy Space Center

I met Kennedy Press Secretary Pierre Salinger (1925–2004) at the opening of the JFK Library, Boston, Massachusetts, 1979

With famous Broward County Sheriff Nick Navarro at my
McDonalds Mall location JFK show, 1985, Pompano Beach, Florida

With TV personality Mary Hart at a children's Christmas party

First public showing of my collection at the Monroe County Fair, 1976

With "Goober," George Lindsey, at my Nashville JFK show

Broward County, Florida Sheriff Nick Navarro
at one of many parades and dedications

Dearborn, Michigan. The original x-100 and the McDonalds "Speedy" sign
on display next to each other. A big part of my life right there!

Kennedy's AF1 #26000 Palm Beach.
Permission granted by Captain of 26000 and the Secret Service!

My 4th grade teacher Mrs. Ruder at Riverside School in Monroe, Michigan presenting me with her book JFK wrote

My Flag Depot Store created in 1994

Kevin MacDonald, Visionary & Builder of the iconic Kennedy Car

DEPARTMENT OF THE NAVY
HEADQUARTERS UNITED STATES MARINE CORPS
WASHINGTON, D.C. 20380-0001

IN REPLY REFER TO

10120
Ser MCUB/129-90

2 8 MAR 1990

Mr. Fred N. Ciacelli
JFK Remembered, inc.
5625 Leitner Drive West
Coral Springs, Florida 33067

Dear Mr. Ciacelli,

    This is in response to your letter of March 21, 1990.
Purchase of one male enlisted dress blue uniform with accessories
has been approved.

    The uniform items you will need may be purchased in person or
by telephone from The Military Clothing Sales Store, Marine Corps
Base, Camp Lejeune, North Carolina. After you receive the
uniform, if you need assistance with the proper manner of wearing
it, we suggest you contact the nearest Marine Corps recruiting
station.

    I am glad that we were able to assist you and wish you
success in your endeavor with establishing the JFK Museum.

                              Sincerely,

                              G. WONG
                              Captain, U.S. Marine Corps
                              Secretary-Recorder, Permanent
                              Marine Corps Uniform Board

Special permission letter from the government

My limo (left) as seen with the
Goodyear Blimp while filming
Speed Channel's *Behind the Headlights*
series. Pompano Beach, Florida

The Kennedy Experience exhibition—
"The museum experience you'll never forget!"
Visit www.JFK35.com

Presidential seal. The eagle's right talon clutches an olive branch and thirteen leaves to represent peace. The left talon clutches arrows, which represent the need sometimes to go to war to protect the nation. The eagle holds a ribbon bearing the words, "E pluribus unum," the motto of the US, which means "out of many, one."

The number thirteen is used to represent the thirteen original colonies. A shield in front of the eagle has thirteen red and white stripes, again representing the colonies, with a blue bar above, representing both the unity of the colonies into one nation and Congress, which makes the laws for all.

Above the eagle is a "glory Or" or halo of gold. In it are thirteen white clouds, thirteen white stars, and many tiny stars. The fifty stars on the field of deep blue circle the eagle and represent the fifty states.

Ingram Content Group UK Ltd.
Milton Keynes UK
UKHW020437310323
419426UK00011B/96

9 798822 906617